W9-AKW-829

good
housekeeping

ALL-TIME FAVORITE RECIPES

good
housekeeping

ALL-TIME FAVORITE RECIPES

Good Housekeeping Books New York

GOOD HOUSEKEEPING BOOKS

Editor MINA WHITE MULVEY
Art Director WILLIAM LEFT
Art Consultant JOHN ENGLISH
Senior Editor PATRICIA DEMPSEY
Copy Editor JUANITA G. CHAUDHRY
Assistant to Art Director LYNN THOMPSON

FOOD PUBLICATIONS DIVISION

Director HEDDA SCHLOSBERG
Consultant DOROTHY B. MARSH
Associate Food Editors MARJORIE GRIFFITHS
                      JEANNE CAMPBELL
Assistant Food Editors EILEEN RUNYAN
                      PATRICIA ASHCROFT

FOR GOOD HOUSEKEEPING MAGAZINE

Editor WADE H. NICHOLS
Executive Editor JOHN B. DANBY
Managing Editor BENSON SRERE
Art Director BERNARD SPRINGSTEEL
Director, The Institute WILLIE MAE ROGERS

All photographs by James Viles
except picture on page 12, by Paul Dome

Copyright © MCMLXXI by The Hearst Corporation. Manufactured in the
United States of America. All rights reserved. No part of this book may
be reproduced in any manner whatsoever without the written permission
of the publisher. ISBN 0-87851-007-9. Library of Congress Catalog
Number 75-175343

contents

appetizers
&
soups

First courses to begin a meal, delicious tidbits for parties, main-dish soups and soups that whet the appetite for what's to come—the best of them all are here

No man has ever proved able to resist these succulent tidbits, marinated in garlic and red wine. Try serving them with warm cocktail rye bread, and see!

KING-SIZE STEAK BITES

seasoned instant meat tenderizer
1 3- to 4-pound round steak,
   cut 1 inch thick
1 cup dry red wine
1 garlic clove, crushed
½ cup butter or margarine

1 tablespoon dry mustard
1 teaspoon Worcestershire
½ teaspoon salt
dash pepper
few drops Tabasco

1

About 2 hours before serving: Apply tenderizer to steak as label directs. Mix wine and garlic and use to marinate steak; cover; chill 1½ hours.

2

Preheat broiler if manufacturer directs. Broil steak about 15 or 20 minutes for medium rare, turning once.

3

Melt butter; add mustard and rest of ingredients plus 2 tablespoons of the marinade. Cut steak into cubes; heap into serving dish; pour on sauce; serve with picks. Makes 12 to 16 appetizer servings.

NIPPY CARROT NIBBLERS

3 tablespoons salad oil
3 garlic cloves, minced
1 tablespoon chopped onion
1 pound medium carrots, thinly
   sliced
¼ cup vinegar

1 tablespoon whole pickling
   spice
1½ teaspoons salt
½ teaspoon dry mustard
⅛ teaspoon pepper
1 onion, thinly sliced

1

Day before: In large skillet, in hot salad oil, sauté garlic and onion about 5 minutes. Add carrots and vinegar.

2

In cheese cloth loosely tie pickling spice; add with salt, mustard and pepper to carrots. Simmer, covered, 5 minutes or until carrots are crisp; discard bag of spice. Pour carrot mixture into shallow dish; top with onion slices. Cover; chill; toss occasionally. Makes 12 servings.

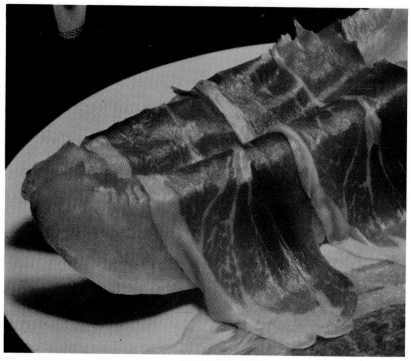

ITALIAN PROSCIUTTO WITH MELON

Prosciutto is Italian-style ham that has been aged in spices to obtain a rich, mellow taste. It comes sliced paper-thin, ready to enhance the melon flavor

ITALIAN PROSCIUTTO WITH MELON

1½ cantaloupes or 1 medium honeydew melon

18 slices prosciutto ham (about ½ pound)

1

About ½ hour before serving: Cut cantaloupes lengthwise into quarters; remove seeds and rind. Cut each of 6 quarters into 2 slices. (Use remaining half melon for fruit cup the next day.) Or, cut honeydew lengthwise in half; remove seeds and rind; cut each half into 6 slices.

2

On each of 6 plates, arrange 2 melon wedges; top with 2 slices of prosciutto; lay 1 slice at the side. Eat with fork and knife, first a piece of melon, then a piece of ham, thus combining the two flavors. Makes 6 servings.

As sumptuous as their name suggests, Oysters Rockefeller take only half an hour to make

---

OYSTERS ROCKEFELLER

---

3 tablespoons butter or
  margarine
½ package frozen chopped
  spinach
1 tablespoon instant minced
  onion
1 bay leaf, finely crumbled
1 tablespoon chopped parsley

½ teaspoon salt
dash cayenne or Tabasco
¼ cup packaged fine bread
  crumbs
18 large or 24 small oysters on
  the half shell
2 bacon slices, cut into bits
grated Parmesan cheese

1

About 25 minutes before serving: Preheat oven to 425° F. In small saucepan, heat butter; add spinach, instant minced onion, bay leaf, parsley, salt, cayenne. Cook, covered, stirring occasionally, until spinach thaws and is heated through. Add bread crumbs and toss well with fork.

2

Place oysters on shells in large shallow pan (if you have rock salt, place layer in pan first to keep oysters from tilting). Spoon spinach mixture over each oyster; dot with bacon; sprinkle with grated cheese. Bake 10 minutes or until bacon is crisp. Makes 18 to 24.

TOASTED CHEESE SQUARES

---

1 1-pound loaf unsliced, day-old
  white bread
butter or margarine, softened

1 cup shredded natural Cheddar
  cheese

1

Early in day: Cut bread into 1-inch cubes (about 12), then butter bread cubes on all sides but one. Roll cubes in cheese and arrange, unbuttered side down, on cake rack; refrigerate.

2

Just before serving: Preheat broiler if manufacturer directs. Set cake rack on cookie sheet; broil about 2 minutes or until cheese melts and browns. Serve at once. Makes 12.

TINY HAM-STUFFED TOMATOES

1 pint cherry tomatoes
2 2¼-ounce cans deviled ham

2 tablespoons sour cream
2 tablespoons horseradish

1

Early in day: Thinly slice tops from tomatoes; discard pulp; drain. Mix ham and rest of ingredients; fill tomatoes; chill. Makes 20.

Feather-light pastry made with cream cheese and filled with chopped mushrooms, minced onions and sour cream. They really do melt in the mouth!

HOT MUSHROOM TURNOVERS

3 3-ounce packages cream
   cheese, softened
butter or margarine, softened
all-purpose flour
½ pound mushrooms, minced

1 large onion, minced
1 teaspoon salt
¼ teaspoon thyme leaves
¼ cup sour cream
1 egg, beaten

1

Early in day: In large bowl, with electric mixer at medium speed, beat cream cheese, ½ cup butter and 1½ cups flour until soft dough forms; wrap dough in waxed paper; chill at least 1 hour.

2

In medium skillet, in 3 tablespoons butter, sauté mushrooms and onion until tender; blend in salt, thyme and 2 tablespoons flour; stir in cream; chill.

3

On floured surface, roll half of dough into 15-inch circle (about ¹⁄₁₆-inch thick) ; cut into twenty 2¾-inch circles. Roll scraps into ball; chill.

4

On one-half of each circle, place teaspoonful of mushroom mixture. Brush edges with egg; fold other half over filling; with fork, press edges together; prick tops to let out steam; place on ungreased cookie sheet. Repeat with rest of dough, scraps, filling. Brush with egg; cover; chill.

5

About 20 minutes before serving: Preheat oven to 450° F. Uncover turnovers; bake 12 minutes or until golden. Makes about 50.

GREEN CHEESE BALL   GOURMET CHEESE BALL
RED CHEESE BALL

T his trio of cheese balls makes a fine accompaniment for drinks, serves as a centerpiece too

---

GREEN CHEESE BALL

¼ pound Danish blue cheese,
  crumbled
1 tablespoon finely chopped
  celery
2 or 3 green onions, chopped

2 tablespoons sour cream
3 5-ounce jars blue-cheese spread
¾ to 1 cup coarsely chopped
  parsley

1

Several days ahead or day before: In large bowl, with electric mixer at medium speed, beat blue cheese with celery, green onions, sour cream and cheese spread until fluffy. Refrigerate mixture overnight. Shape into ball; wrap in foil; refrigerate.

2

Just before serving: Unwrap cheese ball; reshape into ball; roll in parsley. Makes one 3½-inch ball.

GOURMET CHEESE BALL

3 8-ounce packages cream
  cheese, softened
1 cup preserved ginger, drained,

coarsely chopped
1 5-ounce can diced roasted
  almonds

1

Several days ahead or day before: In large bowl, with electric mixer at medium speed, beat cheese with ginger until thoroughly blended. Shape into ball; wrap in foil; refrigerate.

2

About 30 minutes before serving: Unwrap cheese ball. Reshape into ball; roll in diced almonds. Makes one 4½-inch ball.

Although one is called gourmet, the truth is that the other two balls are just as luscious. Serve all three, pair two together, or settle for a single

RED CHEESE BALL

½ pound natural Cheddar
  cheese, finely grated
1 3-ounce package cream cheese,
  softened
¼ cup pitted ripe olives,
  coarsely chopped

3 tablespoons sherry
½ teaspoon Worcestershire
dash each: onion, garlic and
  celery salts
¼ to ½ cup dried beef, coarsely
  chopped

1

Several days ahead or day before: In large bowl, with electric mixer at medium speed, beat cheeses with olives, sherry, Worcestershire and salts; blend thoroughly. Shape into ball; wrap in foil; refrigerate.

2

About 30 minutes before serving: Unwrap cheese ball. Reshape into ball; roll in chopped dried beef. Makes one 3-inch ball.

On a frosty day, courtesy of either the weather or air conditioning, what could be more welcome than a steaming bowl of chowder like this one?

MANHATTAN CLAM CHOWDER

5 *bacon slices, cut into small pieces*
2 *medium onions, chopped*
2 *stalks celery, thinly sliced*
6 *medium carrots, diced*
½ *pound green beans, cut into 1-inch pieces*
2 *medium potatoes, diced*
1 *10-ounce package frozen baby limas*

1 *28-ounce can tomatoes*
1 *teaspoon thyme leaves*
3 *parsley sprigs*
24 *shucked, raw hard-shelled clams with liquid*
3 *tablespoons butter or margarine*
5 *tablespoons flour*
1 *tablespoon salt*
½ *teaspoon paprika*

1

Day before: In large kettle, sauté bacon until crisp. Remove bacon; drain on paper towels. In bacon fat, sauté onions until golden, about 5 minutes. Add reserved bacon, 8 to 10 cups water, celery, carrots, beans, potatoes, limas, tomatoes and thyme. Simmer, uncovered, for about 1 hour.

2

Add parsley; simmer, uncovered, 1 hour longer. Discard parsley.

3

Meanwhile, drain (do not wash) clams, reserving liquid. Cut each clam into pieces (use entire clam). Add liquid from clams to chowder; simmer 10 minutes.

4

In small bowl, blend butter with flour and salt; stir in enough cold water to make a smooth paste. Add slowly to chowder, stirring constantly. Stir in paprika and cut-up clams. Heat chowder to boiling. Cool; cover and refrigerate until needed.

5

About 20 minutes before serving: Remove any fat from chowder. In same kettle, over low heat, bring chowder just to boiling. (If chowder is too thick, add a little water.) Ladle into soup bowls. Makes 6 to 8 main-dish servings.

MANHATTAN CLAM CHOWDER

FISHERMAN'S CHOWDER

1½ pounds haddock, cod or
   flounder fillets
butter or margarine
 12 medium white onions
  4 or 5 potatoes, pared, thinly
   sliced

salt and pepper
3 cups boiling water
1 quart milk, scalded
1 cup evaporated milk, undiluted
1 ripe tomato
assorted crisp crackers

1

About 1 hour before serving: If necessary, skin and bone fish; cut each fillet into 2 or 3 pieces.

2

In 4-quart Dutch oven, in ¼ cup butter, sauté onions until golden; cook, uncovered, for 10 minutes. Add potatoes, 4 teaspoons salt, ½ teaspoon pepper and boiling water. Arrange fish fillets on top; cover; simmer 15 to 20 minutes, or until vegetables are fork-tender. Add milk, evaporated milk, 3 tablespoons butter; *heat, don't boil.*

3

Slice tomato thinly; sprinkle with salt, pepper; float on chowder. Serve with crackers. Makes 4 servings.

Creamy, cool and curry-spiced, vichyssoise proves summer and soup are meant for each other

BLENDER VICHYSSOISE

 1 cup coarsely diced raw
  potatoes
¼ cup chopped green onions
1½ cups chicken broth
 1 cup raw peas

⅛ teaspoon celery salt
⅛ teaspoon curry powder
 1 cup heavy or whipping cream
chopped parsley

1

Day before: In medium saucepan, cook potatoes, green onions, broth and peas, covered, 10 minutes, or until vegetables are barely tender. Place undrained vegetables in electric-blender container; add celery salt, curry powder. Cover; blend until smooth—30 seconds. Remove; stir in cream. Refrigerate.

2

Serve sprinkled with chopped parsley. Makes 4 servings.

T hick with vegetables, a cupful of borscht tempts the appetite, a bowlful makes a meal

OLD-COUNTRY BORSCHT

1-pound beef brisket, cut into
  6 pieces
2 onions, sliced
2 stalks celery, cut into 1-inch
  chunks
4 medium beets, pared, sliced
  (about 2 cups)
4 carrots, thinly sliced (1½
  cups)
1 small head cabbage, cut into

wedges
1 bay leaf
salt
2 beets, coarsely grated (about
  1 cup)
1 6-ounce can tomato paste
  (⅔ cup)
1 tablespoon granulated sugar
2 tablespoons vinegar
1 cup sour cream (½ pint)

1

Day before or early in day: In large kettle, place 6 cups water, beef, onions, celery, sliced beets, carrots, cabbage, bay leaf, 1 tablespoon salt; simmer, covered, about 2 hours.

2

Add grated beets, tomato paste, sugar, vinegar and 2 teaspoons salt. Simmer, covered, 15 to 20 minutes. Cool; refrigerate.

3

Skim fat from soup. Bring soup to boil over medium heat; lower heat; simmer, covered, 10 minutes. Top with sour cream. Makes 6 servings.

FRENCH ONION SOUP

5 tablespoons butter or
  margarine
4 cups thinly sliced large
  onions
¼ teaspoon pepper

5 beef-bouillon cubes
1 teaspoon salt
5 2-inch toast rounds
2 tablespoons grated Parmesan
  cheese

1

About 1 hour before serving: In Dutch oven, in hot butter, sauté onions until golden brown. Add pepper, bouillon cubes, salt and 5⅓ cups water; bring to boil; stir well; simmer, covered, 1 hour. Serve over toast rounds. Sprinkle with cheese. Makes 5 servings.

CURRIED QUICHE APPETIZERS

T̤o each his own—in this case an individual fluted pastry filled with delectable cheese custard. Many stores carry the 3½-inch quiche pans you'll need

CURRIED QUICHE APPETIZERS

Pastry for a 9-inch two-crust pie
  3 tablespons butter or
     margarine, softened
  2 cups diced onions
  1 tablespoon flour
1½ cups shredded natural Swiss

  cheese (about 6 ounces)
  3 eggs
1½ cups light cream
  2 teaspoons curry powder
1½ teaspoons salt

1

About 2 hours before serving: Divide pastry into 2 balls. On lightly floured surface, with stockinette-covered rolling pin, roll out one ball of pastry into large circle about 1/16 inch thick.

2

With 5-inch circle as guide, cut out 4 circles with knife, reserving pastry scraps. Use each circle to line an individual 3½-inch quiche pan; trim.

Repeat with second ball of pastry. Reroll leftover pastry; cut to make a total of 10 circles. With fingers, rub a little butter over bottom of pastry. Place pans on cookie sheets and chill while preparing filling.

3

Preheat oven to 425° F. In medium skillet, in 2 tablespoons butter, cook onions 5 minutes, or until soft; drain on paper towels. On waxed paper, toss flour with cheese. In medium bowl, beat eggs well; stir in cream, curry and salt.

4

Sprinkle about ¼ cup cheese in bottom of each quiche pan; top each with about 1 tablespoon onion. Pour about ¼ cup cream mixture into each pan. Bake 15 minutes. Lower oven heat to 325° F. and bake 30 to 35 minutes longer until knife inserted in center comes out clean.

5

Cool on rack 10 minutes. Carefully loosen edge of each quiche with tip of knife; gently remove from pans. Serve warm (or refrigerate and serve cold). Makes 10 appetizers.

9-INCH PIE VERSION: Prepare recipe as above but use one pastry-lined 9-inch pie plate spread with butter. Bake at 425° F. for 15 minutes, then lower oven heat to 325° F. 50 to 55 minutes. Makes 10 appetizer wedges.

You can cook these in a chafing dish, serve them, pink and delicately fragrant, at the table

---

SHRIMP INEZ

¼ cup butter or margarine
1 garlic clove, minced
½ teaspoon salt
1 teaspoon monosodium glutamate

1½ pounds shelled deveined medium raw shrimp (about 30)
dash pepper
⅓ cup chopped parsley

1

About 15 minutes before serving: In large skillet, melt butter. Add garlic, salt and monosodium glutamate; sauté until garlic is golden. Add shrimp; sauté, stirring constantly, until shrimp are pink, then sprinkle with pepper; add parsley; cook 1 minute longer.

2

Serve right from skillet or in casserole over candle warmer at table, or from chafing dish or electric skillet. Makes 30.

PATE UNDER ASPIC

Liver pâté blended silken smooth with mushrooms, parsley, onion. Serve it with elegance, molded under aspic with a crown of mushroom slices

PÂTÉ UNDER ASPIC

1 envelope unflavored gelatin	salt
¼ cup sherry (optional)	⅛ teaspoon pepper
1 10½-ounce can condensed beef consommé	¼ cup coarsely chopped parsley
½ pound mushrooms, sliced	dash onion salt
butter or margarine	watercress for garnish
1½ pounds chicken livers	crackers and toasted thins

1

Day before serving: Soften gelatin in sherry or cold water. In small saucepan, heat undiluted consommé with ¾ cup water to boiling; remove from heat; stir in softened gelatin until completely dissolved. Pour ¼ cup consommé mixture into 1½-quart mold or mixing bowl. Arrange 6 to 8 mushroom slices in circle on bottom; refrigerate until set. Chill remaining consommé slightly; pour into mold; refrigerate until firm, about 2 hours.

In large skillet, in ¼ cup hot butter, sauté chicken livers with 1¼ teaspoons salt and pepper until tender; pour into medium bowl. In same skillet, in additional ¼ cup hot butter, sauté remaining mushroom slices with ½ teaspoon salt until tender.

3

In covered electric-blender container, blend livers, mushrooms, parsley and onion salt until smooth. (Or, in chopping bowl, chop until very fine and smooth.) Spread mixture over aspic in mold. Chill overnight.

4

Just before serving: With narrow spatula, carefully loosen edge of liver mixture in mold. Dip mold in warm water a few seconds to loosen. Invert platter on top of it; invert both; lift off mold. Garnish with watercress. Serve with crackers. Makes enough for about 40 appetizers.

---

real old-time favorite that can be made ahead, popped in the oven at the last minute

CURRIED TUNA TOASTIES

2 6½- to 7-ounce cans tuna
1 cup mayonnaise
1 teaspoon instant minced onion
1 teaspoon curry powder

2 regular loaves fresh, unsliced
   white bread, crusts removed
butter or margarine, softened
paprika

1

Day before: In bowl, combine tuna, mayonnaise, onion and curry powder until creamy.

2

Lay each loaf on its side, then, starting at bottom, slice off five ½-inch slices lengthwise. Lightly spread 10 slices with butter. Spread each slice with tuna; sprinkle with paprika. Starting at narrow end, roll up each slice; wrap tightly in waxed paper; refrigerate.

3

Just before serving: Preheat broiler if manufacturer directs. Cut each roll into 6 or 7 crosswise slices. Place on cookie sheet. Toast under broiler, turning once. Makes 5 dozen.

W orcestershire, garlic and onion salts, and cereals are the unlikely ingredients of this smash hit on the cocktail circuit. Almonds, pretzels star too

SIX-IN-ONE COCKTAIL HASH

½ cup butter or margarine
1 tablespoon Worcestershire
¼ teaspoon celery salt
¼ teaspoon seasoned salt
¼ teaspoon cayenne
¼ teaspoon onion salt
¼ teaspoon garlic salt
1 cup packaged toasted-oat cereal

2 cups packaged bite-size shredded rice
2 cups packaged bite-size shredded wheat
2 cups packaged bite-size toasted-corn cereal
1 cup very thin pretzel sticks
½ cup slivered almonds

1

Several days ahead: Preheat oven to 250° F. In shallow roasting pan, melt butter; stir in Worcestershire, seasonings, cereals, pretzels and almonds; toss together.

2

Bake about 1 hour or until well heated, stirring occasionally.

3

Serve warm; or cool well, then store in covered container until needed. Makes 2 quarts of nibblers.

CHABLIS-CHEESE DIP

2 4-ounce packages Liederkranz cheese
2 8-ounce packages soft cream cheese

¼ teaspoon celery salt
¼ teaspoon garlic salt
¼ cup chablis

1

About 1 week ahead: In large bowl, with mixer at medium speed, beat Liederkranz cheese until smooth. Beat in cream cheese, celery and garlic salts. Gradually beat in chablis, blending well—about 3 minutes.

2

Spoon cheese mixture into one large, or several smaller very clean containers. Refrigerate. Cover tightly so flavors will be well blended before serving with crisp crackers or raw vegetables. Makes about 3½ cups.

salads
&
vegetables

Some of these are almost a meal in themselves, others are meant to complement the main dish. All have been singled out, over the years, as very special

CAESAR SALAD

1 garlic clove
salad oil
2 cups ¼-inch bread cubes
3 quarts bite-size pieces romaine
   and iceberg lettuce
¼ cup grated Parmesan cheese
¼ cup crumbled Danish blue
   cheese

1 tablespoon Worcestershire
¾ teaspoon salt
¼ teaspoon freshly ground black
   pepper
1 egg
¼ cup lemon juice
8 anchovies, cut up (optional)

1

Early in day: Preheat oven to 300° F. Quarter garlic; drop into ¼ cup oil; set aside. Toast bread cubes in shallow pan 20 minutes, or until golden; toss often with fork. Place lettuce in salad bowl; refrigerate.

2

Just before serving: Sprinkle greens with cheeses; drizzle on ½ cup salad oil mixed with Worcestershire, salt, pepper. Toss gently until every leaf glistens. Break whole raw egg onto greens; pour lemon juice over all; toss until egg specks disappear.

3

Remove garlic from ¼ cup oil; pour over bread cubes; toss. Sprinkle bread and anchovies over greens. Toss salad; serve at once. Makes 4 or 5 servings.

This salad, invented by a literary agent, may keep his memory greener than his clients'

MAX'S SPINACH-BACON SALAD BOWL

6 garlic cloves, quartered
¾ cup French dressing
2 quarts crisp young spinach

3 eggs, hard cooked
8 bacon slices, cooked

1

2 hours ahead: Add garlic to French dressing. In salad bowl, tear spinach into pieces; refrigerate all.

2

At serving time: Chop eggs; crumble bacon; sprinkle both over spinach. Remove garlic from French dressing, then pour it over salad; toss; serve at once. Makes 6 servings.

CURRIED CHICKEN SALAD

Lovely to look at and heaven to eat—a spiced chicken mixture piled high in pineapple shells and served with the traditional curry accompaniments

CURRIED CHICKEN SALAD

7 cups cooked rice
1 cup raw cauliflowerets, cut in ¼-inch slices
1 8-ounce bottle creamy style French dressing
1 cup mayonnaise or salad dressing
1 tablespoon curry powder
1 tablespoon salt
½ teaspoon pepper

½ cup milk
7 cups cooked chicken or turkey, in large chunks (6 pounds uncooked)
1 cup thin green-pepper strips
2 cups celery, cut on angle
1 cup thinly sliced red onions
pineapple shells or romaine lettuce

1

Early in day: Toss rice with raw cauliflowerets and French dressing; cover and refrigerate at least 2 hours.

2

In large bowl, combine mayonnaise, curry powder, salt and pepper;

slowly stir in milk; add chicken; toss. Cover; refrigerate at least 2 hours.

3

Just before serving: In large bowl, combine rice mixture with chicken mixture, then add green pepper, celery and onions.

4

Serve in pineapple shells or turn out onto platter lined with romaine leaves. Makes 12 servings. Nice served with some or all of the Curry Accompaniments (below).

CURRY ACCOMPANIMENTS: Flaked coconut, canned French-fried onion rings, salted peanuts, currant jelly and tomato wedges. Or, you may add one or all of these: chutney, raisins, chopped parsley, crisp bacon bits, chopped hard-cooked eggs, sweet or sour pickles, sliced avocados or grated orange peel.

T his salad was first served to San Franciscans, who promptly called it divine. Everyone does

GREEN GODDESS SALAD

1 garlic clove, minced	*green onions*
½ teaspoon salt	*⅓ cup chopped parsley*
½ teaspoon dry mustard	*1 cup mayonnaise*
1 teaspoon Worcestershire	*½ cup sour cream*
2 tablespoons anchovy paste	*⅛ teaspoon black pepper*
3 tablespoons tarragon-wine	*1 quart salad greens*
vinegar	*olives for garnish*
3 tablespoons minced chives or	

1

Early in day: In bowl or jar, combine all ingredients except salad greens and olives, until well blended; refrigerate, covered, until needed. Makes 1⅓ cups.

2

At serving time: Place greens in salad bowl. Pour about ⅓ cup dressing over them. Toss well, then serve at once; garnish with stuffed olives if desired. Makes 4 servings.

T

he toast of two continents—a spicy-sweet salad that originally came to us from Australia. Three kinds of beans contribute to the mixture of flavors

TWENTY-FOUR-HOUR BEAN SALAD

1 15½-ounce can cut wax beans, drained
1 16-ounce can French-style green beans, drained
1 17-ounce can kidney beans, drained
1 cup thinly sliced onions

½ cup salad oil
½ cup cider vinegar
¾ cup granulated sugar
½ teaspoon salt
¼ teaspoon pepper
1 head curly chicory

1

Day before serving: In large bowl, combine all beans with onions. In jar, combine oil, vinegar, sugar, salt and pepper; shake until well blended. Pour this dressing over beans; cover; refrigerate; toss occasionally.

2

Arrange chicory on large platter. Drain dressing from bean mixture; pile beans lightly on chicory. (Or, arrange chicory on individual salad plates and spoon on about ½ cup beans.) Makes 12 servings.

HEARTS-OF-PALM SALAD

2 heads Boston lettuce
1 14-ounce can hearts-of-palm, drained
1 ripe avocado, peeled, diced

2 tablespoons vinegar
¼ cup salad oil
½ teaspon salt
dash pepper

1

About 15 minutes before serving: Tear lettuce into bite-size pieces; place in very large salad bowl. Slice hearts-of-palm ¼-inch thick; add to greens with avocado.

2

In small jar, combine vinegar, salad oil, salt and pepper; shake well. Pour over salad; toss and serve. Makes about 6 servings.

COLONEL'S LADY'S SALAD BOWL

¾ cup salad oil
½ cup vinegar
3 tablespoons granulated sugar
3 tablespoons chopped parsley
1½ teaspoons garlic salt
1½ teaspoons salt
1 teaspoon monosodium glutamate
¾ teaspoon oregano leaves
½ teaspoon pepper

1½ 10-ounce packages frozen green peas
6 quarts mixed greens (lettuce, curly endive, romaine), cut in bite-size pieces
1½ large cucumbers, thinly sliced
9 green onions (tops and all), chopped
3 stalks celery, sliced diagonally

1

Up to 1 week ahead: In covered 1-pint jar, mix salad oil with next 8 ingredients; refrigerate.

2

Just before serving: Place frozen peas in medium bowl; cover with boiling water; drain at once. In large salad bowl, toss peas with all vegetables. Shake vinegar-and-oil mixture well; pour over salad; toss well. Makes 12 servings.

Bananas, strawberries and pineapple all lurk beneath the "frosting" of this gelatin delight

FROSTED FRUIT SALAD

2 3-ounce packages strawberry gelatin
2 cups boiling water
1 10-ounce package frozen strawberries

2 large ripe bananas, mashed
1 15¼-ounce can crushed pineapple
1 cup sour cream

1

Day before serving: In large bowl, combine gelatin and boiling water; stir to dissolve gelatin; stir in strawberries until they are thawed. Stir bananas and pineapple into gelatin. Pour into 8-inch springform pan or 13" by 9" baking pan. Refrigerate until set.

2

Just before serving: Spread with sour cream. Makes 12 servings.

NOODLES ALFREDO

N oodles with a difference—in this case, a whisper of garlic and a sprinkle of chopped nuts

NOODLES ALFREDO

2 8-ounce packages medium
 noodles
½ garlic clove
¾ cup butter or margarine
1¼ cups light cream

1 cup shredded or grated
 Parmesan cheese
¾ teaspoon seasoned pepper
2 tablespoons finely chopped
 walnuts

1

About 20 minutes before serving: Cook medium noodles as package label directs until barely tender; drain.

2

With garlic, rub skillet. In it, place butter, light cream, cooked noodles; set over direct heat. (Or, place ingredients in blazer of chafing dish, with heat source lighted.) Simmer all for 1 minute, tossing gently with fork and spoon. Mix in Parmesan, pepper and nuts until just blended. Serve immediately. Makes 4 servings.

COMPANY WILD RICE

1 cup uncooked wild rice	1 10½-ounce can condensed
salt	cream-of-mushroom soup
2 tablespoons butter	1 cup heavy cream
¼ cup minced onion	¼ teaspoon dried marjoram
2 tablespoons minced green	dash dried basil
pepper	dash dried tarragon
1 3- or 4-ounce can sliced	½ teaspoon curry powder
mushrooms, drained	¼ teaspoon pepper

1

About 40 minutes before serving: Wash rice well in cold water. To 3 cups boiling water in saucepan, add 1 teaspoon salt; stir in rice. Cover; simmer 30 minutes or until rice is tender and water is absorbed.

2

Meanwhile, in another saucepan, in 2 tablespoons hot butter, sauté onion, green pepper and mushrooms 5 minutes. Stir in undiluted soup, ½ teaspoon salt, cream and rest of ingredients; heat 10 minutes. Add cooked wild rice; heat, stirring occasionally. Makes 4 servings.

Clever, those Chinese! Look at the way they cook asparagus, juicy and tender, in 5 minutes

CHINESE ASPARAGUS

1½ pounds fresh asparagus	½ teaspoon salt
3 tablespoons butter	dash pepper

1

About 20 minutes before serving: Wash asparagus. With knife, remove scales that hold sand and grit. Lay 2 asparagus stalks together on cutting board; with sharp knife, cut slices, on the diagonal, not more than ¼ inch apart and 1½ inches long.

2

In large skillet with tight cover, put butter and ¼ cup water; heat. Add asparagus, salt, pepper. Cover; cook over high heat 5 minutes, shaking skillet occasionally and checking once to see if more water is needed. Test asparagus with fork; if not tender-crisp, cook 1 minute more. Serve at once. Makes 4 servings.

EGGPLANT PARMIGIAN

1 egg
2 tablespoons water
1 medium eggplant, cut crosswise
   into ½-inch slices
½ to ¾ cup packaged dried
   bread crumbs
salad oil

1 8-ounce can tomato sauce
½ teaspoon oregano
½ teaspoon Italian seasoning
½ teaspoon dried savory
½ cup grated Parmesan cheese
8 slices mozzarella cheese

1

About 1 hour before serving: Preheat oven to 375° F. Beat egg with water. Dip eggplant slices into egg mixture, then into bread crumbs.

2

In large skillet, in ¼ cup salad oil, sauté a few of the eggplant slices until they are brown on outside and fork-tender. Repeat, using more salad oil each time, until rest of slices have been sautéed.

3

Lightly grease a 2-quart casserole. In it, arrange half of eggplant, then half of tomato sauce, oregano, Italian seasoning, savory, Parmesan and mozzarella; repeat layers. Bake 30 to 40 minutes. Makes 4 to 6 servings.

Plain old peas never tasted like this, and no wonder. Sherry, mushrooms and spices are the ingredients that turn an everyday dish into a gourmet special

PEAS CONTINENTAL

2 tablespoons butter or
   margarine
1 cup drained canned sliced
   mushrooms
¼ cup minced onion
¼ teaspoon salt

dash pepper
¼ teaspoon nutmeg
⅛ teaspoon dried marjoram
2 tablespoons sherry (optional)
2 cups drained hot cooked peas

1

About 10 minutes before serving: In medium skillet, in butter, sauté mushrooms and onion until onion is tender. Add salt, pepper, nutmeg, marjoram and sherry. Stir in peas; heat through. Makes 4 servings.

EGGPLANT PARMIGIAN

P

otato pancakes are hearty enough to be a main dish. Or serve as marvelous go-alongs

---

POTATO PANCAKES

---

5 tablespoons flour
1½ pounds potatoes, pared
1 small onion
1 egg

1 teaspoon salt
⅛ teaspoon pepper
salad oil

1

About 30 minutes before serving: To prevent darkening, plan to fry pancakes as soon as mixture is made. Measure flour into bowl. Over flour, grate potatoes on very fine grater; grate in onion; stir in egg, salt and pepper.

2

Lightly grease medium skillet; place over medium heat. Drop potato mixture, by heaping tablespoonfuls, into hot skillet. Fry until crisp and golden-brown on underside; turn; brown other side, adding more oil as needed. Drain on paper towels.

3

Serve as vegetable with pot roast, short ribs, etc. Or, serve with applesauce as luncheon or supper main dish. Makes about 16 pancakes.

CHINESE CAULIFLOWER

---

1 small to medium head crisp,
  firm cauliflower
salt
2 tablespoons butter or

margarine
2 tablespoons heavy cream
paprika

1

About 15 minutes before serving: Wash and remove lower stalks from cauliflower. With coarse shredder, shred entire head; or, with sharp knife, slice each floweret thinly. Place in skillet; sprinkle lightly with salt; add ⅓ cup hot water. Cook, covered, 5 to 7 minutes or until slightly crisp; do not drain. Add butter and cream; heat, tossing with fork, 1 to 2 minutes. Sprinkle with paprika. Makes 3 or 4 servings.

GNOCCHI AU GRATIN

4 cups cold mashed potatoes (2 to 2½ pounds potatoes)
1½ cups all-purpose flour
6 egg yolks
2 teaspoons salt
¼ teaspoon pepper
1 teaspoon prepared mustard
5 2½-ounce jars shredded Parmesan cheese
1 tablespoon salt
½ cup melted butter or margarine

1

About 40 minutes before serving: Preheat oven to 350° F. In large bowl, combine mashed potatoes, flour, egg yolks, 2 teaspoons salt, pepper, mustard and 4 jars of the cheese.

2

Meanwhile, in large kettle, bring 6 quarts of hot water to simmering; add 1 tablespoon salt. In large pastry bag fitted with plain tube no. 8 put some of potato mixture. Holding bag over water, force out ¾-inch pieces of gnocchi; cut with scissors. Cook gently. As gnocchi rise, remove at once with slotted spoon; drain well on paper towels; place in buttered 1½-quart shallow casserole; keep in warm oven. Repeat with remaining dough until all is used. Remove casserole from oven; preheat broiler if manufacturer directs. Pour butter over gnocchi; sprinkle with remaining cheese. Broil until golden—about 5 minutes. Makes 12 servings.

Creamy melted marshmallows fill the centers of these orange-flavored, delicately crisp morsels

SWEET-POTATO SURPRISES

1 18-ounce can vacuum-packed sweet potatoes
⅓ cup milk
1 tablespoon butter
½ teaspoon salt
⅛ teaspoon pepper
1 teaspoon grated orange rind
4 marshmallows
1 egg, beaten
1 cup crushed cereal flakes

1

About 30 minutes before serving: Preheat oven to 425° F. In saucepan, place sweet potatoes, milk, butter; heat till butter is melted. Mash potatoes; add salt, pepper, orange rind. Form into 4 balls, with marshmallow in center of each. Be sure marshmallows are completely covered. Roll balls in egg, then in cereal. Bake in pie plate 20 to 25 minutes or until crusty. Makes 4 servings.

A perfect accompaniment for almost any main dish, with a spicy tang that tempts the palate

---
CURRIED-FRUIT BAKE
---

1 16-ounce can cling-peach halves
1 20-ounce can sliced pineapple
1 16-ounce can pear halves
5 maraschino cherries with stems

⅓ cup butter
¾ cup packed light brown sugar
4 teaspoons curry powder

1

Early in day: Preheat oven to 325° F. Meanwhile, drain fruits and dry well on paper towels; arrange in 1½-quart casserole.

2

Melt butter; add brown sugar and curry; spoon over fruit. Bake 1 hour, uncovered; refrigerate.

3

30 minutes before serving: Reheat casserole in 350° F. oven 30 minutes. Serve warm with ham, lamb, poultry. Makes 12 servings.

ENDIVES AU FOUR
---

18 Belgian or French endives
salt
¼ cup butter or margarine, cut
   in small pieces

¾ pound natural Swiss cheese,
   coarsely grated
pepper
½ cup light cream

1

Early in day: Wash endives. With tip of knife, remove small core from root end of each. Place endives in saucepan; cover with boiling water; add 1 teaspoon salt; cover; simmer 20 minutes. Drain; chill.

2

About 40 minutes before serving: Preheat oven to 350° F. In greased 12″ by 8″ by 2″ baking dish, arrange half of endives. Top with half of butter and cheese. Sprinkle lightly with salt and pepper. Repeat. Pour cream over all. Bake 20 minutes or until cheese is melted. Raise oven heat to "Broil"; place endives under broiler for 3 minutes or until cheese is bubbling. Makes 6 servings.

CURRIED-FRUIT BAKE

BEANS TRÈS BIEN

2 9-ounce packages frozen French-
   style green beans
1 10½-ounce can condensed

cream-of-mushroom soup
1 3½-ounce can French-fried
   onions

1

30 minutes before serving: Preheat oven to 400° F. Cook green beans 1 minute less than label directs, then drain off all but ½ cup liquid. Turn beans into 1½-quart casserole; stir in undiluted soup and onions. Bake about 10 minutes or until bubbly. Makes 4 servings.

No short-cut methods here. The beans soak overnight, bake all day. They're worth it

OLD-FASHIONED BOSTON BAKED BEANS

1 pound pea or navy beans
2 teaspoons dry mustard
pepper
 1 tablespoon salt
 3 medium onions, quartered
¼ cup packed brown sugar

¼ cup molasses
 2 tablespoons sweet pickle
   juice; or 2 tablespoons
   vinegar, with dash ground
   cinnamon and cloves
¼-pound piece salt pork

1

Night before: Pick over beans; wash; place in large pot; cover with 3 cups water; soak 8 hours or overnight.

2

Early in day: To beans, add 2 cups water, mustard, ¼ teaspoon pepper and next 5 ingredients. Boil, covered, about 1 hour, or until skins wrinkle.

3

Preheat oven to 250° F. Cut salt pork at ½-inch intervals almost all the way through; place in 2-quart bean pot; add hot beans and their liquid, covering pork; sprinkle with pepper. Bake 6 hours, covered, or until tender.

4

When beans are two thirds baked, add about ¾ cup water, or enough to just cover. Uncover last ½ hour. Makes 4 to 6 servings.

main

dishes

The best of show—from simple but delectable dishes for family meals to the spectacular kind that demand a whole tableful of guests to do them justice

A true spectacular, Beef Wellington deserves an occasion when the people you most want to impress can admire its glorious flavor, golden puff pastry

BEEF WELLINGTON

3 cups sifted all-purpose flour
1 teaspoon salt
butter
3 or 4 large pieces of suet
5- to 6-pound fillet of beef
4 chicken livers
½ pound fresh mushrooms,

finely chopped
¼ pound cooked ham, finely ground
1 tablespoon catchup
⅓ cup sherry
1 egg, separated

1

3 days before serving: Make puff pastry. Sift flour into large bowl, make well in center; pour in ¾ cup water and 1 teaspoon salt. With fork, quickly mix together, adding ½ cup more water as it is absorbed into flour; chill 15 minutes. On lightly floured surface roll pastry into rectangle ¼ inch thick. Shape 1½ cups firm, but not hard, butter into flat square cake 1 inch thick; place in center of pastry; fold pastry over it like an envelope. Roll into thin rectangle, taking care not to let butter break through. Fold into thirds, then refold resulting rectangle into thirds. (This is a "turn.") Do 2 more turns. Chill 20 minutes. Do 2 more turns; chill 30 minutes. Repeat turns twice more; wrap in foil; chill.

2

Day before serving: Preheat oven to 425° F. Place suet over fillet. In shallow roasting pan, roast to desired degree of doneness—140° F. for rare (about 40 minutes). Remove suet; cool; refrigerate.

3

In skillet, in 2 tablespoons butter, sauté chicken livers until browned; chop fine. In same skillet, sauté mushrooms, ham, catchup and sherry 10 minutes; stir occasionally. Cool; stir in beaten egg yolk; remove to bowl; cover; refrigerate.

4

About 1 hour before serving: On floured surface, roll three fourths of puff pastry into 18-inch square or one large enough to enclose fillet. Lay bottom of fillet along one edge of pastry. Pat chicken-liver mixture on top of fillet. Lift pastry up and over fillet; tuck in all ends; place, seam side down, on cookie sheet. Preheat oven to 425° F. Brush pastry with slightly beaten egg white. Bake 30 to 40 minutes or until golden. Makes fourteen ½-inch servings.

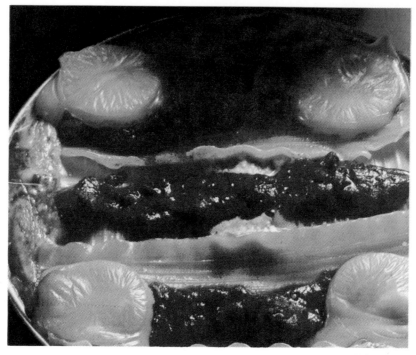

LASAGNA

Th*here is ordinary lasagna, and
then there is this superb recipe, a step-by-step guide to a classic

---

LASAGNA

¾ *pound beef chuck, ground*
¼ *pound boned pork shoulder,
  ground*
4 *eggs*
1 *cup grated Parmesan cheese*
¾ *cup packaged dried bread
  crumbs*
chopped parsley
salt
1 *pound sweet or hot Italian
  sausages*
2 *garlic cloves, minced*

1 *6-ounce can tomato paste*
3 *29-ounce cans Italian-style
  tomatoes (10 cups)*
½ *teaspoon fennel seed*
1 *teaspoon dried basil*
1 *pound lasagna noodles*
3 *pounds ricotta cheese*
½ *to 1 teaspoon freshly ground
  black pepper*
1 *pound mozzarella cheese,
  sliced*

1

Day before: Make meatballs: Mix chuck, pork, 2 of the eggs, 2 tablespoons Parmesan cheese, crumbs, 1 tablespoon parsley, 1 teaspoon salt;

divide in half. Shape half of mixture into 10 large meatballs; shape rest into about 4 dozen tiny balls.

2

In Dutch oven, brown sausages with 1 garlic clove until some fat collects. Add meatballs, a few at a time; brown. Remove garlic, sausages and meatballs.

3

To fat in Dutch oven, add tomato paste; cook over low heat a few minutes. Add tomatoes, 1 tablespoon salt, fennel seed; simmer, uncovered, stirring frequently, about 1 hour or until very thick. Add sausages, meatballs, 2½ cups water; cook slowly, uncovered, about 2 hours. Remove sausages and large meatballs from sauce. Cool, then refrigerate all.

4

About 2 hours and 30 minutes before serving: Reheat lasagna sauce (with tiny meatballs) over low heat until sauce bubbles. Add 2 tablespoons parsley, garlic and basil; then remove 1 cup sauce, add it to the large meatballs and sausages; refrigerate. In open roasting pan, measuring 15½″ by 10½″ by 2½″, spread one fourth remaining meatball sauce. Preheat oven to 400° F.

5

Cook lasagna noodles as label directs. Quickly drain noodles and immediately hang them over side of colander for easier handling. Place about one third of lasagna noodles, one at a time, over sauce in pan until bottom is covered.

6

Blend well ricotta, 2 eggs, ¼ cup parsley, 1 tablespoon salt, pepper; spread half of this mixture over noodle layer; sprinkle with one-third of Parmesan cheese and one third of mozzarella. Repeat layers once more (sauce, noodles, ricotta mixture, Parmesan and mozzarella). Top with one-fourth sauce and noodles. Sprinkle top with remaining Parmesan cheese; spread rest of sauce over entire surface, and dot with remaining mozzarella.

7

Bake lasagna 1 hour. Remove from oven; let stand 15 to 30 minutes for easier cutting. Meanwhile, slowly reheat reserved sausages and large meatballs in sauce; add a little water if necessary. Pass with lasagna. Makes 12 servings.

GINGER BEEF

2 onions
3 garlic cloves
1½ teaspoons turmeric
¼ teaspoon dried chili peppers
(optional)
5 teaspoons powdered ginger
1½ teaspoons salt
1¼-pound flank steak, cut

diagonally across grain, into
thin slices or 2" by ½" strips
3 tablespoons peanut or salad
oil
1 29-ounce can tomatoes
1 10½-ounce can condensed
onion soup

1

Early in day: In chopping bowl, combine onions, and next five ingredients; chop fine. Add steak; toss together. Refrigerate 3 hours.

2

About 2 hours before serving: In Dutch oven, in oil, brown steak and onion mixture; add tomatoes. Cook, uncovered, over high heat, 10 minutes. Add undiluted soup; cover and simmer 1 hour if steak is sliced, 1½ to 2 hours if cut in strips (or until steak is tender) . Nice over rice. Makes 4 servings.

FONDUE BOURGUIGNONNE

about 3 cups salad oil
3 pounds beef tenderloin or tips
of tenderloin, cut into bite-size
cubes
Horseradish Sour Cream Sauce

(below)
Herb Butter Sauce (below)
Spicy Steak Sauce (below)
Mild Mustard Sauce (below)

1

Early in day: Prepare the sauces; refrigerate.

2

About 15 minutes before serving: Heat enough salad oil to fill fondue pan or chafing dish to a depth of 1½ inches. Divide beef among 6 or 8 plates.

3

At serving time: Remove sauces from refrigerator. Each person spears a cube of meat on long fondue or cooking fork, plunges it into hot salad oil in fondue pan, cooks it to desired doneness (about 1 minute or so) , then transfers it to dinner fork and dips it into one of the sauces. Makes 6 to 8 servings.

HORSERADISH-SOUR-CREAM SAUCE: Stir 1½ teaspoons horseradish into ½ cup sour cream; refrigerate. Garnish with chopped chives. Makes ½ cup.

HERB BUTTER SAUCE: In small saucepan, combine 1 tablespoon minced shallots or onion, 1 teaspoon dried tarragon and ⅔ cup red wine. Boil over medium heat until liquid is reduced to about ¼ cup; let cool. In small bowl, with electric mixer at medium speed, cream ½ cup butter or margarine until fluffy; beat in cooled wine mixture, 1 tablespoon chopped parsley, ¼ teaspoon salt and ⅛ teaspoon pepper; chill. Makes ½ cup.

SPICY STEAK SAUCE: Combine ⅓ cup mayonnaise, 3 tablespoons chili sauce, 2 teaspoons Worcestershire, 1 teaspoon bottled thick meat sauce and several dashes Tabasco; stir until smooth; refrigerate. Makes ½ cup.

MILD MUSTARD SAUCE: Stir 2 tablespoons prepared mustard into ½ cup bottled coleslaw dressing; refrigerate until serving time. Makes ½ cup.

O f all the meatball recipes we have ever offered, this wine-flavored version is the most popular

BURGUNDY MEATBALLS

¾ pound chuck, ground	¾ cup light cream
¾ cup packaged dried bread crumbs	salt
1 small onion, minced	¼ cup salad oil
¾ teaspoon cornstarch	3 tablespoons flour
dash allspice	1 cup Burgundy wine
1 egg, beaten	2 beef-bouillon cubes
	⅛ teaspoon pepper

1

About 1 hour before serving: In bowl, combine meat, crumbs, onion, cornstarch, allspice, egg, cream, ¾ teaspoon salt; shape into 30 to 32 small balls. Into hot oil in skillet, drop balls, a few at a time; brown well; remove; keep warm.

2

Blend flour with remaining oil in skillet; stir in 2 cups water, wine, bouillon cubes, ½ teaspoon salt, pepper. Cook, stirring, until smooth. Then arrange meat balls in sauce; simmer, covered, 30 minutes. Makes 6 servings.

A dish that lives up to its name, Imperial Ham requires some time to bake, but little to prepare

IMPERIAL HAM

1 15-pound fully cooked smoked
   ham
prepared mustard
2 packages piecrust mix for 9-inch

double crust pie
2 egg yolks
watercress

1

Early in day: Preheat oven to 325° F. Remove all skin and excess fat from ham down to 3 inches from shank end. In large shallow roasting pan, bake ham for 1½ hours; refrigerate.

2

About 2 hours before serving: Preheat oven to 325° F. Brush ham generously with prepared mustard. Make up piecrust mixes as label directs; on floured surface with floured rolling pin, roll out dough into circle ⅛ inch thick. Carefully lay circle over top of ham, trimming sides so bottom of ham is uncovered; press pastry to ham.

3

Form pastry trimmings into ball; roll out ⅛ inch thick; then, with 1-inch round cookie cutter, cut 18 pastry circles. Now, with thumb and forefinger, pinch each of 5 pastry circles into petal shape; group them together into posy, right on ham, as pictured. Nearby, make and arrange 2 more posies in spray effect, using 15 of the 18 pastry circles in all. With same cookie cutter, cut a "first-quarter" moon shape from each of 3 pastry circles, leaving 3 leaf-shape pieces. Now, with palms of hands, roll pastry scraps into rope, ⅛ inch thick. Arrange this rope on ham in stemlike pattern, as pictured, and attach the 3 leaves; gently press all of them to ham.

4

In small bowl, beat egg yolks with 1 teaspoon water; use to brush entire pastry cover and trimmings. Then bake ham 1½ hours.

5

Serve it on platter, garnished with watercress. Pass prepared mustard, if desired. Makes 45 servings.

IMPERIAL HAM

With cranberry-apple stuffing and a garnish of cherry tomatoes, this roast will grace any holiday table. But don't save it just for special occasions

HOLIDAY CROWN ROAST OF PORK

½ cup butter or margarine
2 onions, chopped
3 cups chopped celery
8 cups day-old bread cubes
2 teaspoons salt
1 teaspoon poultry seasoning
¼ teaspoon pepper
2 cups cranberries, chopped

4 cups sliced, pared apples
crown roast of pork (2 half-loin crowns of 13 ribs each)
seasoned salt
ground sage
apricot preserves, melted
cherry tomatoes for garnish
watercress for garnish

1

About 6 hours before serving: In small skillet, in butter, sauté onions until brown. In large bowl, combine celery and next 6 ingredients with onions.

2

Preheat oven to 325° F. Place roast, rib ends up, in large shallow roasting pan, without rack. Lightly sprinkle with seasoned salt and sage. Fill center of crown with stuffing. With foil, loosely cover stuffing and also tightly cover rib ends.

3

Insert roast-meat thermometer, between two ribs, into center of meat (don't touch bone or stuffing). Roast pork about 2 hours and 15 minutes; or until thermometer reads 165° F. Remove foil.

4

Brush all surfaces with melted apricot preserves, and return to oven for 30 minutes, or until thermometer reaches 170° F. With the help of 2 large spatulas or pancake turners, carefully lift roast to a heated serving platter. Let roast stand 15 minutes.

5

Press a cherry tomato on each or on alternate rib ends. Garnish base with watercress and cherry tomatoes.

6

To serve: Allow 2 ribs per serving. Spoon some stuffing onto each plate, too. Makes about 13 servings.

LAMB CHOPS HARBERT

4 2-inch-thick loin lamb chops
1 garlic clove, cut
salt
pepper

monosodium glutamate
1/4 pound Roquefort cheese
1 teaspoon Worcestershire
hot pepper sauce

1

About 30 minutes before: Preheat broiler if manufacturer directs. Rub each lamb chop with garlic; then sprinkle with salt, pepper and mono-sodium glutamate. Broil chops, 10 minutes on each side for medium, 12 to 14 minutes on each side for well done.

2

Meanwhile, blend cheese, Worcestershire and hot pepper sauce. A few minutes before chops are done, spread surface of each with 2 table-spoons Roquefort mixture; finish broiling. Makes 4 servings.

What is better than a good steak? One with a blue-cheese topping, broiled until golden

DOUBLE-THICK RARE STEAK

1 porterhouse steak, 3 inches
    thick
1 garlic clove, cut
1/2 cup crumbled Danish blue
    cheese
1/4 cup butter or margarine,

softened
1 teaspoon salt
1/2 teaspoon pepper
1 teaspoon Worcestershire
1 tablespoon prepared mustard
1 tablespoon lemon juice

1

About 45 minutes before serving: Preheat broiler if manufacturer di-rects. Rub steak with garlic. Broil steak about 25 minutes on first side, or until browned. Turn; broil 25 minutes. Cut steak near bone and check doneness. Broil longer if necessary.

2

Meanwhile, cream together blue cheese and rest of ingredients. Spread cheese mixture on steak; broil 5 minutes more or until topping is golden. Makes 8 servings.

VEAL PARMIGIAN

T he Italian way with veal—combine it with tomatoes, onion, garlic, and native cheeses

VEAL PARMIGIAN

olive or salad oil
  3 garlic cloves, finely minced
  1 onion, minced
  1 16-ounce can tomatoes
1¼ teaspoons salt
  ¼ teaspoon pepper
  1 8-ounce can tomato sauce
  ¼ teaspoon thyme leaves
  1 egg

  ¼ cup packaged dried bread
      crumbs
  ½ cup grated Parmesan cheese
  1 pound thin veal cutlets, cut
      into 8 pieces about 4½" by
      2"
  ½ pound mozzarella or Muenster
      cheese

1

About 1 hour before serving: In saucepan, in 3 tablespoons hot oil, sauté garlic and onion until golden. Add tomatoes, salt, pepper; break up tomatoes with spoon; simmer, uncovered, 10 minutes. Add tomato sauce, thyme; simmer, uncovered, 20 minutes.

Beat egg well with fork. Combine crumbs, ¼ cup Parmesan cheese. Dip each veal piece into egg, then into crumbs. In skillet, in 1 tablespoon hot oil, sauté a few pieces at a time, until golden brown on both sides. Repeat until all are done. Set slices side by side in 12″ by 8″ by 2″ baking dish.

3

Preheat oven to 350° F. Thinly slice mozzarella. Pour two thirds of tomato mixture over veal, straining it, if desired. Arrange mozzarella on top; spoon on rest of tomato mixture. Sprinkle with ¼ cup Parmesan. Bake, uncovered, 30 minutes or until meat is fork-tender. Makes 4 generous servings.

Again the meat is veal cutlet, but now it is filled with Swiss cheese and ham, then browned and simmered until tender in a beef-and-wine-flavored gravy

CUTLET OF VEAL À LA SUISSE

about 1½ pounds thin veal
   cutlets (6)
6 thin slices Swiss cheese
6 paper-thin slices cooked ham
2 tablespoons flour
½ teaspoon paprika

⅓ cup butter or margarine
1 cup sauterne or Rhine wine
1 cup canned beef gravy
½ cup light cream
dash salt
1 teaspoon lemon juice

1

About 45 minutes before serving: Using edge of heavy saucer, pound cutlets well; halve each. On each of 6 cutlet halves, place ½ slice cheese, 1 slice ham folded over, then another ½ slice cheese. Cover each with second cutlet half. Fasten securely with wooden picks. Coat lightly with flour mixed with paprika.

2

In skillet, in hot butter, brown cutlets. Add ½ cup wine; simmer, uncovered, until liquid is almost absorbed. Add remaining wine, gravy, cream; simmer, covered, 10 minutes or until fork-tender. Just before serving, add salt, lemon juice; remove picks. Makes 6 servings.

VEAL PAPRIKA

2 tablespoons bacon fat or
   shortening
2-pound boned veal shoulder,
   cut into 1-inch cubes
1 teaspoon monosodium
   glutamate
2 beef-bouillon cubes
3½ cups boiling water

1 medium onion, thinly sliced
1 teaspoon salt
¼ teaspoon pepper
2 teaspoons paprika
1⅓ cups uncooked regular rice
1 3- or 4-ounce can sliced
   mushrooms
1 pint sour cream

1

About 1½ hours before serving: In Dutch oven, in hot bacon fat, brown veal; sprinkle with monosodium glutamate.

2

Dissolve bouillon cubes in boiling water; add to veal, along with onion, salt, pepper, paprika. Simmer, covered, 45 minutes. Add rice, mushrooms with liquid; stir well; simmer, covered, 25 minutes or until rice is done. Remove from heat. Stir in sour cream. Add salt if needed. Makes 8 servings.

A veal dish that saves pennies but doesn't skimp on taste uses a less expensive cut, extends it with rice, in a tasty combination of mushrooms and onions

VEAL SCALLOPINI

2½ pounds boned veal shoulder,
   cut into 1¼-inch cubes
½ cup flour
salt
pepper
½ cup salad oil

½ cup minced onions
¾ cup canned whole or sliced
   fresh mushrooms
1¾ cups canned tomato juice
1 teaspoon sugar
hot fluffy rice

1

About 2 hours before serving: Preheat oven to 350° F. Roll veal lightly in flour mixed with ½ teaspoon salt, ⅛ teaspoon pepper. In skillet, in hot salad oil, sauté onions until tender; remove onions to greased 2-quart casserole.

2

Sauté veal in remaining oil until brown on all sides. Place veal in casserole, along with mushrooms, tomato juice, sugar, 1½ teaspoons salt, ⅛ teaspoon pepper. Bake, covered, 1½ hours or until fork-tender. Spoon over hot rice. Makes 6 servings.

C ook these on a grill if you like—indoors or out, their spicy goodness is simply irresistible

VEAL CHOPS INVERNESS

4 loin veal chops, ¾ inch thick
2 garlic cloves, crushed
salad oil
3 tablespoons soy sauce

2 tablespoons catchup
1 tablespoon vinegar
¼ teaspoon black pepper

1

Day before or early in day: In shallow baking pan, blend garlic with ⅓ cup oil, soy sauce, catchup, vinegar and pepper. Lay chops in this mixture; turn to coat well. Cover pan; refrigerate. Turn chops occasionally while they marinate.

2

About 35 minutes before serving: In skillet over medium heat, in 2 tablespoons hot salad oil, sauté chops for 15 minutes on each side or until nicely browned and fork-tender. Spoon marinade left in pan over them; heat. Makes 4 servings.

VEAL STEAK INVERNESS: Substitute 2-pound veal steak, ¼ inch thick, for chops. Cut steak into serving-size pieces. Marinate and proceed as above. Especially nice served over hot buttered rice which has been tossed with a generous amount of chopped parsley.

SPICED POT ROAST

2 garlic cloves
seasoned salt
5-pound boned beef rump
3 tablespoons salad oil
3 onions, sliced
5 teaspoons chili powder
½ teaspoon ground cumin

½ teaspoon ground coriander
⅓ cup canned tomato paste
1 beef-bouillon cube
1 16-ounce can whole tomatoes
6 cups cooked rice
1 cup canned red kidney beans
avocado wedges for garnish

1

About 3 hours before dinner: Mash garlic with 2 teaspoons seasoned salt. Cut holes in rump and fill them with garlic mixture.

2

In Dutch oven, in hot salad oil, brown rump; add onions; sauté until golden. Add ½ teaspoon seasoned salt, chili powder and next 4 ingredients. Add liquid drained from tomatoes plus enough water to make 1¼ cups. Simmer, covered, 2½ hours or until almost tender. Add tomatoes and simmer about 15 minutes or until rump is tender. Arrange rump on platter; top with some of gravy; pass rest. Toss together rice and beans. Place around meat with avocado. Makes 10 servings.

M ignonettes" means "little darlings," and that's just what these steak tidbits are. First the meat is tenderized, then wrapped in bacon for extra flavor

BROILED FLANK STEAK MIGNONETTES

1 2-pound flank steak, trimmed
  of fat
seasoned instant meat

tenderizer
¼ teaspoon seasoned pepper
6 bacon strips

1

About 1 hour before serving: Preheat broiler if manufacturer directs. Cut off thin tail from steak. With sharp knife, score one side of steak in diamond pattern; sprinkle with tenderizer and pepper. Roll steak up lengthwise; wrap bacon strips around roll; secure with wooden picks. Slice roll between bacon strips into 6 mignonettes. Broil, 8 minutes on one side, and 5 minutes on the other, or to desired doneness. If bacon is not crisp, stand mignonettes on edge and broil them a minute, turning them as they brown. Makes 6 servings.

SPICED POT ROAST

MARTHA'S COMPANY CASSEROLE

1 8-ounce package noodles
butter or margarine
1 pound beef chuck, ground
2 8-ounce cans tomato sauce
½ pound cottage cheese (1 cup)
1 8-ounce package cream cheese,

softened
¼ cup sour cream
⅓ cup chopped green onions
1 tablespoon chopped green
pepper

1

About 45 minutes before serving: Preheat oven to 375° F. Cook noodles as label directs; drain. In skillet, in 1 tablespoon butter, sauté chuck until browned. Stir in tomato sauce. Remove from heat. Combine cottage cheese and next 4 ingredients. In 2-quart casserole, spread half of noodles; cover with cheese mixture, then with rest of noodles. Pour on 2 tablespoons melted butter, then meat mixture. Bake, uncovered, 30 minutes. Makes 6 servings.

E ven without the Hungarian name, this recipe's origin is made obvious by its characteristic combination of paprika and sour cream. Lemon adds zest

BRAISED SIRLOIN ESTERHÁZY

6 sirloin steaks, about ½ pound
each, ¼-inch thick
1 tablespoon salt
1 teaspoon pepper
3 tablespoons butter or
margarine
6 carrots, pared, cut in strips
8 celery stalks, cut in strips
6 onions, peeled, sliced

3 tablespoons flour
6 whole peppercorns
1 tablespoon paprika
1 10½-ounce can condensed
beef bouillon
6 bottled capers
1 lemon, thinly sliced
1½ cups sour cream

1

About 2 hours before serving: Lay meat on board; with rim of saucer, pound in salt and pepper on both sides.

2

In large skillet, in hot butter, brown meat on both sides. Remove from skillet, and set aside. In remaining butter, sauté carrots, celery and onions about 15 minutes, stirring occasionally. Stir in flour, then peppercorns, paprika, undiluted bouillon.

Return meat to skillet; cover; simmer 30 minutes, or until vegetables and meat are tender. Add capers, lemon. Cook, uncovered, about 15 minutes or until liquid is reduced one third. Dilute sour cream with about 1 cup of liquid in skillet; stir into mixture in skillet. Heat thoroughly, but do not boil. Makes 6 servings.

BOEUF BOURGUIGNON

5 pounds chuck, cut into 2-inch cubes	2 cups coarsely chopped onions
flour	chopped parsley
butter or margarine	2 bay leaves
¼ teaspoon pepper	1 teaspoon thyme leaves
¼ cup cognac	1½ cups Burgundy
½ pound bacon slices, diced	1 cup sweet sherry
4 garlic cloves, minced	2 pounds small white onions
2 carrots, coarsely chopped	sugar
2 leeks, coarsely chopped	2 pounds fresh mushrooms
	2 teaspoons lemon juice

1

Day before: Roll beef cubes in ⅓ cup flour. In Dutch oven, in ¼ cup hot butter, brown meat very well; sprinkle with pepper; pour on cognac; ignite with match; let flame die out. Preheat oven to 350° F. To beef, add bacon, garlic, carrots, leeks, chopped onions, 1 tablespoon chopped parsley, bay leaves, thyme, 1 cup of the Burgundy, sherry. Bake, covered, 2 hours or until beef is fork-tender; remove meat from Dutch oven. Put all vegetables and liquid through coarse strainer or food mill, mashing vegetables as you strain. Return strained liquid and meat to Dutch oven; chill.

2

About 45 minutes before serving: Reheat meat mixture in Dutch oven over low heat. In skillet, in 2 tablespoons butter, brown whole onions; add 1 teaspoon sugar, remaining ½ cup Burgundy; cook, covered, 15 to 20 minutes, or until onions are tender, adding ¼ cup water if needed; add to meat, with liquid and 1 tablespoon sugar.

3

In skillet, in 2 tablespoons butter, sauté half of mushrooms until golden; sprinkle with 1 teaspoon lemon juice; add to meat mixture. Repeat with rest of mushrooms. Makes 12 servings.

A smash-hit company casserole you can prepare ahead, pop into the oven shortly before your guests arrive. Almonds add texture to its distinctive taste

SHRIMP CASSEROLE HARPIN

2½ pounds raw shrimp, shelled, deveined
1 tablespoon lemon juice
3 tablespoons salad oil
¾ cup uncooked regular rice
2 tablespoons butter or margarine
¼ cup chopped green pepper
¼ cup chopped onion

1 10½-ounce can condensed tomato soup
1 teaspoon salt
⅛ teaspoon pepper
⅛ teaspoon mace
dash cayenne pepper
1 cup heavy or whipping cream
½ cup sherry
¾ cup slivered blanched almonds

1

Early in day: Cook shrimp in boiling salted water for 5 minutes; drain. Place in 2-quart casserole; sprinkle with lemon juice and salad oil. Meanwhile, cook rice as label directs; drain. Refrigerate all.

2

About 1 hour before serving: Preheat oven to 350° F. Set aside 8 shapely shrimp for garnish. In skillet, in butter, sauté green pepper and onion for 5 minutes. Add to shrimp in casserole, along with rice, undiluted soup, next 6 ingredients and ½ cup of the almonds. Mix well. Bake, uncovered, 35 minutes. Top with reserved shrimp and ¼ cup almonds. Bake 20 minutes longer or until mixture is bubbly. Makes 6 to 8 servings.

SHRIMP WITH DILL SAUCE

⅓ cup butter or margarine
⅓ cup flour
2¼ teaspoons salt
1¼ teaspoons dill weed

4 cups milk
6 cups cooked medium shrimp (about 2½ pounds shelled)
toast points

1

About 20 minutes before serving: In medium saucepan over medium heat, melt butter and blend in flour, salt and dill. Slowly add milk, stirring constantly, until smooth and thickened; add shrimp; serve over toast points. Makes 8 servings.

SHRIMP CASSEROLE HARPIN

LOBSTER THERMIDOR ON CURRIED RICE

I s it the tender, juicy lobster that makes this dish a favorite? The sherry-flavored, nutmeg-flecked sauce? The curried rice and chutney? Does it matter?

LOBSTER THERMIDOR ON CURRIED RICE

6 8-ounce frozen rock-lobster
    tails
butter or margarine
1/4 cup flour
1/8 teaspoon nutmeg
paprika
  1 teaspoon salt
  3 tablespoons sherry

2 cups light cream
2 cups uncooked regular rice
1 tablespoon curry powder
2 medium onions, minced
1/4 cup shredded process Cheddar
    cheese
chutney

1

Early in day: Cook lobster tails in boiling salted water to cover (1 teaspoon salt per 1 quart water), allowing 3 minutes, or longer than the ounce weight of largest tail. Drain; cool.

2

With scissors, cut thin underside membrane; pull out meat; cut into chunks. Wash, then reserve shells. Refrigerate all.

About 1 hour before serving: In 2-quart double boiler, melt 6 table-spoons butter; stir in flour, nutmeg, dash of paprika, salt and sherry. Slowly add cream, stirring constantly; then add lobster chunks. Cook over hot water, stirring occasionally, until just thickened. Meanwhile, preheat oven to 400° F. Make Curried Rice: In skillet, in ¼ cup butter, brown rice lightly; place it in 2-quart casserole. Stir in curry powder and minced onions. Pour on 1 quart boiling water. Bake, covered, 30 to 35 minutes, or until tender and all water is absorbed.

Preheat broiler if manufacturer directs. Fill reserved shells with hot lobster mixture. Sprinkle each with some shredded cheese and then lightly with paprika. Arrange filled shells in foil-lined jelly-roll pan; broil until just golden on top. Arrange lobsters on serving platter with Curried Rice. Garnish with chutney. Makes 6 servings.

For 12 servings: Double all ingredients.

---

 seafood dish with a double promise—sole stuffed with a shrimp-and-mushroom mixture

STUFFED FILLETS OF SOLE

2 tablespoons butter
2 4½-ounce cans shrimp, drained
1 3- or 4-ounce can mushrooms, chopped, drained
1 large onion, minced
2 tablespoons chopped parsley
8 sole fillets (about 3 pounds)

½ teaspoon salt
pepper and paprika
2 10½-ounce cans condensed cream-of-mushroom soup
⅓ cup sherry
½ cup shredded process Cheddar cheese

1

Early in day: In skillet, in hot butter, sauté shrimp, mushrooms, onion and parsley until onion is soft. Sprinkle both sides of each fish fillet with salt, pepper and paprika. Onto one end of each fillet, spoon some of onion mixture, then roll up fillet, securing with wooden pick; place in 12″ by 8″ by 2″ baking dish. In medium bowl, combine undiluted soup, ¼ cup water and sherry; pour over fillets; sprinkle with cheese; refrigerate.

2

About 40 minutes before serving: Preheat oven to 400° F. Sprinkle fillets and sauce with paprika. Bake 30 minutes or until fish flakes easily with fork. Makes 4 to 6 servings.

T

he scallop is a dainty thing,
And subtle is its savor. But for dishes fit to feed a king,
You can scarcely beat its flavor." Especially in this dish

SEAFOOD SUPREME

½ pound scallops (1 cup)
¼ cup butter or margarine
3½ tablespoons flour
¼ teaspoon salt
dash pepper
½ cup light or heavy cream
½ cup milk
1 teaspoon paprika

½ teaspoon Worcestershire, or
   sherry to taste
dash cayenne pepper
1 cup cooked, cleaned shrimp
1 dozen oysters, drained
   (about 1 pint)
1 cup cooked crab

1

About 45 minutes before serving: Cook scallops in 1 cup boiling, salted water, covered, 10 minutes; drain.

2

Melt butter in double boiler. Add flour, salt, pepper; blend well. Slowly add cream and milk, stirring; cook over boiling water until thickened, stirring occasionally. Blend in paprika, Worcestershire and cayenne pepper; cover, then cook 10 minutes over medium heat. Add scallops and shrimp; cook 15 minutes. Add oysters and crab; cook 10 minutes, stirring occasionally. Makes 6 servings.

CRAB IMPERIAL

---

6 tablespoons butter
¼ cup chopped green pepper
½ cup flour
1½ teaspoons dry mustard
1½ teaspoons salt
1½ teaspoons Worcestershire
⅛ teaspoon paprika

⅛ teaspoon pepper
3 cups milk
¼ cup lemon juice
3 egg yolks, beaten
2 1-pound packages frozen
   Alaska King crab, thawed,
   drained

1

About 1½ hours before serving: Preheat oven to 350° F. In large saucepan over medium heat, melt butter and cook green pepper until tender, about 5 minutes. Stir in flour, mustard, salt, Worcestershire, paprika and pepper until smooth. Continue cooking and slowly add milk, stirring constantly, until sauce thickens and comes to a boil. Remove from heat and stir in lemon juice, a few spoonfuls at a time.

2

In cup, combine about ¼ cup sauce with egg yolks. Slowly stir egg mixture into sauce and blend well; fold in crab.

3

Pour mixture into greased 2½-quart casserole. Bake 1 hour or until golden on top. Makes about 12 servings.

Besides tasting absolutely delicious, this casserole has the virtue of stretching the lobster

---

JANE'S COMPANY LOBSTER

3 cups cut-up, cooked or canned lobster meat	¼ teaspoon dry mustard
3 tablespoons lemon juice	¾ teaspoon salt
½ teaspoon mace	dash pepper
¼ pound elbow macaroni (1 cup)	2 cups milk
1 teaspoon minced onion	½ pound process Cheddar cheese, shredded (2 cups)
2 tablespoons butter	¼ cup sherry
1 tablespoon flour	⅓ cup crushed, crisp round scalloped crackers

1

About 45 minutes before serving: Preheat oven to 400° F. Sprinkle lobster with lemon juice, mace. Cook macaroni as label directs; drain.

2

In double boiler, combine onion, butter, flour, mustard, salt, pepper; stir in milk. Cook, stirring, until smooth. Add 1½ cups of the cheese; stir until melted. Add lobster, sherry.

3

Arrange macaroni in 12″ by 8″ by 2″ baking dish; pour on lobster mixture; sprinkle with rest of cheese, then with crackers. Bake, uncovered, 20 minutes, then remove from oven and let stand in warm place 5 minutes before serving. Makes 4 to 6 servings.

A fish stew, streamlined for American cooks, that has all the flavor of the French original

BOUILLABAISSE À L'AMÉRICAINE

olive or salad oil
3 large onions, chopped
2 large green peppers, chopped
3 large carrots, chopped
30 to 50 small hard-shell clams in shell, scrubbed
4 small whole fish, boned and cleaned (bonito, mackerel, bluefish or sea bass)
1 to 2 pounds large raw shrimp,
shelled if desired
3 live lobsters, split, with claws cracked
2 tablespoons salt
1/2 to 1 teaspoon pepper
2 loaves French bread, cut in 1-inch slices
melted butter or margarine
garlic salt
chopped parsley for garnish

1

About 45 minutes before serving: In each of two 8-quart kettles heat 3/4 cup oil. To each, add half of onions, peppers, carrots; over medium heat, brown lightly.

2

Then in one kettle arrange clams; top with whole fish, each cut in half; in second kettle arrange shrimp, then top with lobsters. To each kettle, add about 2 1/2 cups water, 1 tablespoon salt and 1/4 to 1/2 teaspoon pepper. Cover kettles tightly; bring mixture to boil; reduce heat, cook 10 to 20 minutes or until clams open, lobsters are red, fish flakes easily.

3

Meanwhile, preheat oven to 425° F., then toast bread and brush with melted butter seasoned with garlic salt.

4

To serve: Carefully arrange the clams, shrimp, lobsters and fish on separate heated platters or in casseroles; sprinkle with parsley. Serve broth in bowl or casserole, bread in basket. Makes 8 to 10 servings. Don't forget to pass hot, moist finger-tip towels, paper napkins or towelettes.

GOURMET STYLE: Substitute dry white wine for 1 cup water; add 1/2 teaspoon each dried thyme leaves and sage. Pass chunks of warm crusty French bread.

ROCK CORNISH HENS ON RICE MINGLE

8 frozen Rock Cornish hens
   (about 1 pound each), thawed
salt
pepper
soft butter or margarine

paprika
¼ cup melted butter or
   margarine
Rice Mingle (below)
Bordelaise Sauce (opposite)

1

Early in day: Remove giblets from hens; rinse body cavities; pat dry. Sprinkle hens with salt and pepper; with thin string, tie legs together. Rub hens with soft butter; sprinkle with paprika. Place in shallow roasting pan; refrigerate.

2

About 1 hour and 15 minutes before serving: Preheat oven to 425° F. Roast hens, uncovered, about one hour or until tender and well browned, basting frequently with melted butter.

3

Meanwhile, start Rice Mingle; also prepare step 1 of Bordelaise Sauce.

4

When hens are done, cut strings. Arrange around edge of heated serving platter; fill center with Rice Mingle; keep warm. Complete Bordelaise Sauce as in steps 2 and 3 of recipe. Makes 8 servings.

Like many good things, wild rice is expensive. Stretch it by mixing it with regular rice

RICE MINGLE

1 cup wild rice
salt
2 cups boiling water
butter or margarine
2 medium onions, minced

2 10½-ounce cans condensed
   beef consommé
2 cups uncooked regular rice
dash pepper

1

About fifty minutes before serving: Wash wild rice in 3 or 4 changes of cold water, removing foreign particles.

In medium saucepan, add 1 teaspoon salt to boiling water; add wild rice gradually so water keeps boiling. Boil, covered, stirring occasionally with fork, 30 to 45 minutes or until rice is just tender.

3

Meanwhile, in large, deep 10-inch skillet over medium heat, in ¼ cup butter, sauté onions about 5 minutes; stir in consommé, 1 soup-can water, regular rice and ½ teaspoon salt. Cover skillet tightly. Bring mixture to boiling, reduce heat, then simmer about 20 minutes or until rice is tender and all liquid absorbed. Four or five times during cooking, stir rice with fork to prevent sticking.

4

To drained wild rice, add 1 tablespoon butter and dash pepper. Then, with fork, fluff it up and toss together with regular rice.

5

Heap this Rice Mingle lightly on heated serving platter, mounding in center, and surround with Rock Cornish hens, if desired. Makes about 8 servings.

BORDELAISE SAUCE FOR ROCK CORNISH HENS

½ teaspoon dried whole thyme
1 bay leaf
1 cup port wine
2 chicken-bouillon cubes
⅓ cup boiling water

1 tablespoon cornstarch
2 teaspoons sugar
½ cup hot drippings
1 medium onion, chopped

1

In small bowl, combine thyme, bay leaf and wine; set aside. Dissolve bouillon cubes in boiling water; quickly stir in cornstarch and sugar; set aside.

2

When Cornish hens have been arranged on serving platter, pour ½ cup of the hot drippings from roasting pan into small skillet. In drippings, sauté onion 5 minutes; stir in cornstarch mixture and bring to boiling. Stir in port wine and simmer 5 minutes. Strain sauce into sauceboat. Makes 8 servings.

This one is a hearty country-man's dish, chockful of chicken, ham, vegetables and hard-cooked eggs and topped with a crust that bakes golden-crisp

BOER CHICKEN PIE

2 3-pound stewing chickens, quartered	¼ pound cooked ham, sliced, then quartered
salt	4 hard-cooked eggs, sliced
1 teaspoon whole allspice	¼ cup butter or margarine
1 teaspoon peppercorns	¼ cup flour
3 bay leaves	⅓ cup sherry
3 medium carrots, cut ½ inch thick	2 tablespoons lemon juice
3 celery stalks, cut ½ inch thick	¼ teaspoon mace
	¼ teaspoon pepper
3 medium onions, quartered	2 egg yolks
10 parsley sprigs	pastry for 9-inch two-crust pie
	1 egg, beaten

1

Early in day or day before: In large kettle, bring chickens to a boil in 1 quart water with 1 tablespoon salt, allspice, peppercorns and bay leaves. Add carrots, celery, onions and parsley; simmer, covered, ½ hour or until vegetables are tender-crisp. Strain broth; reserve 2 cups. Remove skin from chickens; cut meat from chicken in chunks. In 12″ by 8″ by 2″ baking dish, arrange chicken, carrots, celery, onion, ham and eggs.

2

In saucepan, melt butter; stir in flour, 1 teaspoon salt; gradually add chicken broth, sherry and next 3 ingredients. Cook, stirring, until thickened. Beat egg yolks and slowly stir into sauce; heat, stirring con-stantly, until thickened. Do not boil. Pour sauce over chicken. Roll pastry into 14″ by 10″ rectangle; place over chicken. Trim pastry, leaving ½-inch overhang. Turn under; press firmly to edge of dish; make scalloped edge.

3

In center of top crust, with knife, cut out rectangle 7″ by 3″. At each corner of rectangle make ½-inch diagonal slit; turn pastry edges up to form scalloped edge. With remaining dough and small cookie cutter, cut out small designs; arrange on pastry; refrigerate.

4

About 45 minutes before serving: Preheat oven to 425° F. Brush pie with beaten egg. Bake 30 minutes or until pastry is golden. Makes 8 servings.

BOER CHICKEN PIE

CHICKEN WITH HERBS EN CASSEROLE

2 tablespoons bacon fat
1 4-pound roasting chicken, cut up
butter or margarine
6 tablespoons flour

3 cups milk
2½ teaspoons salt
⅛ teaspoon pepper
¾ teaspoon thyme leaves
¾ teaspoon dried sage

1

About 2 hours before serving: In heavy skillet, in bacon fat, cook chicken pieces, a few at a time, turning occasionally with tongs until golden.

2

Preheat oven to 325° F. Arrange chicken pieces, side by side, in 12″ by 8″ by 2″ baking dish or 2-quart casserole.

3

Measure drippings left in skillet; add enough butter to make ½ cup. Pour back into skillet; add flour; blend until smooth. Then stir in milk, salt, pepper, thyme and sage; cook until smooth and thickened. Pour sauce over chicken. Bake, uncovered, about 1 hour or until fork-tender. Makes 6 servings.

A luncheon delicacy—chicken suspended in the amber gelatin of its own concentrated broth

PRESSED CHICKEN

2 4-pound roasting chickens
1 cup sherry
1 carrot, pared, sliced
1 cup sliced celery
1 leek, halved lengthwise
2 bay leaves
¼ teaspoon whole cloves
1 teaspoon dried savory

parsley
1 garlic clove, halved
¾ cup minced onions
¼ teaspoon whole peppercorns
1 tablespoon salt
watercress, parsley or curly chicory for garnish

1

Day before serving: In large kettle, place chickens, 1 quart water, sherry, sliced carrot, celery, leek, bay leaves, cloves, savory, 10 parsley sprigs, garlic, onions, peppercorns, salt. Simmer, covered, 2 hours or until chicken is tender. Remove chicken to tray; cool. Skim fat from cooled broth; strain broth through fine sieve into large saucepan. Boil, uncovered, until 2 cups liquid remain.

2

When chicken is cool, remove meat from bones in large-size pieces. Add chicken to broth; simmer, covered, 10 minutes. Stir in 3 tablespoons chopped parsley. In 10″ by 5″ by 3″ loaf pan, arrange chicken lengthwise in layers; pour on broth. Fill another loaf pan about three-fourths full with cold water. Place on top of chicken to weigh it down. Refrigerate overnight.

3

Just before serving: With spatula, loosen chicken from sides of pan, then dip pan part-way in and out of warm water. Unmold on serving platter. Garnish with watercress, parsley or curly chicory. Makes 8 servings.

STIR-FRY CHICKEN

2 tablespoons salad oil
2 whole chicken breasts, skinned, boned, cut into 1/4-inch strips
1 green pepper, cut in strips
1 small onion, sliced 1/4 inch thick
1 cup celery strips
1 5-ounce can water chestnuts, drained, sliced
1/2 cup chicken broth
1 teaspoon monosodium glutamate
1 teaspoon salt
1/4 teaspoon ginger
2 teaspoons cornstarch
2 tablespoons soy sauce
1 16-ounce can bean sprouts, drained

1

About 15 minutes before serving: In heavy skillet over medium high heat, heat salad oil. Add chicken strips and cook, stirring with fork, until they turn white—about 3 minutes. Add green pepper and next seven ingredients. Cover; cook 7 minutes.

2

Mix cornstarch with soy sauce until smooth. Add to skillet with bean sprouts. Turn down heat and simmer chicken mixture, uncovered, 3 minutes, stirring occasionally. Serve immediately, while chicken is crisp. Nice with hot rice or noodles. Makes 4 servings.

CHICKEN ESPAÑOL

Chicken parts are simmered with tomatoes and green peppers in this Spanish-inspired dish, then tossed with macaroni and garnished with seafood

CHICKEN ESPAÑOL

⅓ cup flour
seasoned salt
  1 teaspoon paprika
¼ teaspoon pepper
  6 each: chicken drumsticks, thighs, wings
butter or margarine
  1 large green pepper, seeded, slivered
  1 26-ounce can whole tomatoes, drained, chopped

  1 teaspoon monosodium glutamate
  1 16-ounce package large macaroni shells
¼ teaspoon dried saffron
  1 9-ounce package frozen artichoke hearts
12 cherrystone clams, in shells
½ pound fresh shrimp, shelled, deveined

1

About 2½ hours before serving: Combine flour, 2 teaspoons seasoned salt, paprika, pepper; use to coat all chicken pieces.

In 8-quart Dutch oven, in ¼ cup melted butter, sauté chicken until golden; to it, add green pepper, tomatoes and monosodium glutamate. Cook, covered, over medium heat, 45 minutes; stir occasionally.

3

Preheat oven to 375° F. Boil macaroni shells as label directs, but only until partially tender; drain. Mix saffron with 2 tablespoons hot water; stir into macaroni; toss with chicken in Dutch oven; bake, uncovered, 30 minutes.

4

While chicken bakes, cook artichoke hearts as label directs; also, steam clams in a little water until their shells open—about 10 minutes.

5

In 2 tablespoons melted butter, sauté the shrimp until pink and tender —about 3 to 5 minutes; sprinkle with ½ teaspoon seasoned salt.

6

To serve: Arrange macaroni and chicken on platter; garnish with artichokes, clams and shrimp. Makes 8 servings.

Done to a turn in the same skillet, golden chicken is complemented by tender shrimp

CHICKEN AND SCAMPI

1 3½-pound broiler-fryer, cut up	3 tablespoons chopped parsley
1 tablespoon salt	½ cup port wine
½ teaspoon pepper	1 8-ounce can tomato sauce
¼ cup butter or margarine	1 teaspoon dried basil
3 small onions, finely chopped	1 pound raw shrimp, shelled,
1 garlic clove, minced	deveined

1

About 45 minutes before serving: Rub chicken well with salt and pepper. In large skillet, in hot butter, sauté chicken until golden. Add onions, garlic, 3 tablespoons chopped parsley, wine, tomato sauce and basil; simmer, covered, about 30 minutes or until chicken is tender.

2

Push chicken to one side of skillet; turn up heat so tomato mixture boils; add shrimp; cook, uncovered, 3 minutes or until just pink. Skim off any fat. Makes 6 servings.

This dish was named for a famous singer, who is said to have eaten it after every performance. It's a velvety blend of chicken, mushrooms, spaghetti, cream

CHICKEN TETRAZZINI

1 4½-pound roasting chicken, cut up
salt
1 teaspoon onion salt
½ teaspoon celery salt
½ pound spaghettini
6 tablespoons butter or margarine

½ pound mushrooms, sliced
1 tablespoon lemon juice
2 tablespoons flour
paprika
¼ teaspoon pepper
⅛ teaspoon nutmeg
1 cup heavy or whipping cream
⅔ cup grated Parmesan cheese

1

Day before or early in day: In deep kettle, place chicken, 3 cups hot water, 2 teaspoons salt, onion salt and celery salt. Simmer, covered, about 1 hour or until fork-tender. Remove chicken meat in big pieces from bones; cut chicken breast into thirds. Refrigerate.

2

From deep kettle, remove and reserve 2½ cups chicken broth. Add 3 quarts water and 2 tablespoons salt to rest of broth. Bring to boil; slowly add spaghettini (water should not stop boiling) and cook, stirring occasionally, 6 minutes; drain; place in 12″ by 8″ by 2″ baking dish.

3

Meanwhile, in medium skillet, in 3 tablespoons butter, sauté mushrooms, sprinkled with lemon juice and ½ teaspoons salt, until soft but not brown. Toss them and their butter with spaghettini; cover; refrigerate.

4

In saucepan, melt 3 tablespoons butter; remove pan from heat; stir in flour, ¼ teaspoon paprika, 1½ teaspoons salt, pepper and nutmeg. Slowly stir in the 2½ cups reserved broth (¼ cup sherry may replace ½ cup broth). Cook sauce, stirring, until thickened; add cream; pour over refrigerated chicken. Cover; refrigerate.

5

½ *hour before serving:* Heat oven to 400° F. Coat chicken and spaghettini thoroughly with sauce and place in baking dish; sprinkle all with Parmesan cheese, paprika. Bake 25 minutes. Makes 8 servings.

CHICKEN CACCIATORE

6 tablespoons salad oil
2 2½- to 3-pound broiler-fryers,
 cut up
1 cup minced onions
1 cup minced green peppers
4 garlic cloves, minced
1 29-ounce can tomatoes (3½
 cups)

1 8-ounce can tomato sauce
½ cup Chianti wine
3¾ teaspoons salt
½ teaspoon pepper
½ teaspoon allspice
2 bay leaves
½ teaspoon thyme leaves
dash cayenne pepper

1

About 1 hour before serving: In large skillet, in hot oil, sauté chickens until golden on all sides. Add onions, green peppers, garlic; brown lightly. Add tomatoes, tomato sauce, wine, salt, pepper, allspice, bay leaves, thyme, cayenne pepper. Simmer, uncovered, 30 to 40 minutes or until chicken is fork-tender. Makes 8 servings.

Spicy yet sweet, with a hint of lemon, this makes a perfect basting mixture for chicken, fish, lamb, or almost anything else you have a yen to barbecue

BERT'S SUPERB BARBECUE SAUCE

¼ cup vinegar
2 tablespoons sugar
1 tablespoon prepared mustard
½ teaspoon pepper
1½ teaspoons salt
¼ teaspoon cayenne pepper

1 thick lemon slice
1 onion, sliced
¼ cup butter or margarine
½ cup catchup
2 tablespoons Worcestershire

1

In saucepan, mix vinegar, ½ cup water, sugar, mustard, pepper, salt, cayenne, lemon, onion, butter. Simmer, uncovered, 20 minutes. Add catchup and Worcestershire; bring to boil. Use for basting when broiling or roasting chicken, fish, or lamb. Makes about 1¾ cups.

BREAST OF CHICKEN PÉRIGOURDINE

8 whole chicken breasts
1 13¾-ounce can chicken broth
¼ cup dried mushrooms*
2 canned truffles, cut up
3 tablespoons dry sherry
butter or margarine

8 large fresh mushrooms, sliced
⅓ cup flour
¼ teaspoon salt
2 tablespoons light cream
Hollandaise Sauce (below)

1

About 1½ hours before serving: Bone chicken breasts, reserving bones; simmer bones in chicken broth, covered, about 1 hour; discard bones; reserve broth. Soak mushrooms in ½ cup water and truffles in sherry.

2

In large, metal-handled skillet, in small amount of hot butter, gently brown chicken breasts, adding more butter as needed; remove. In same skillet, in more butter, sauté fresh mushrooms until golden; remove.

3

Into drippings in same skillet, stir flour, salt, dried mushrooms plus their liquid, 1 cup chicken broth and cream. Cook over medium heat, stirring, until thickened and smooth. Place chicken breasts in sauce; simmer gently, covered, about 20 minutes or until chicken is tender; add truffles, sherry, cooked fresh mushrooms. Preheat broiler if manufacturer directs. Then, over chicken, spread Hollandaise; run under broiler until golden. Serve at once. Makes 8 servings.

*If you can't buy dried mushrooms you may use 4 extra fresh mushrooms and increase the chicken broth to 1½ cups.

Only Hollandaise, smooth and golden, is worthy of accompanying Chicken Périgourdine

HOLLANDAISE SAUCE

2 egg yolks
¼ teaspoon salt
dash cayenne

½ cup butter or margarine,
melted
1 tablespoon lemon juice

1

In small bowl, with electric mixer at high speed, beat yolks with salt and cayenne until thick; add ¼ cup butter, 1 teaspoon at a time, beating constantly. Combine remaining ¼ cup butter and lemon juice; slowly add, about 2 teaspoons at a time, to yolk mixture, beating constantly. Chill.

ROAST DUCKLING WITH ORANGE GLAZE

1 4- to 5-pound duckling
1 teaspoon caraway seed
1 quart day-old bread crumbs
salt
¼ cup minced onions
¼ cup minced green pepper
½ cup minced celery

⅛ teaspoon pepper
1 tablespoon crushed sage
⅓ cup packed brown sugar
⅓ cup granulated sugar
1 tablespoon cornstarch
1 tablespoon grated orange rind
1 cup orange juice

1

About 3 hours before serving: Preheat oven to 325° F. Sprinkle cavity of duckling with caraway seed. Combine bread crumbs, 1 teaspoon salt and next 5 ingredients; use to stuff bird. Fasten neck skin to back; close body opening and tie leg ends. Roast 2½ to 3 hours or until tender.

2

Meanwhile, in saucepan, combine brown sugar, granulated sugar and cornstarch. Add orange rind and juice and ¼ teaspoon salt; stir until sugar dissolves. Simmer, stirring, until thickened. Makes 1½ cups.

3

To serve: With kitchen scissors and sharp knife, quarter duckling; arrange with stuffing on platter. Pour on some orange glaze; pass rest. Makes 4 servings.

triumph of the French cuisine, this tender roast duckling is served with a sauce that combines the giblet broth with wine and dark sweet cherries

CANETON MONTMORENCY

1 4- to 5-pound duckling,
    quartered
salt
duckling giblets and neck
1 16-ounce can pitted, dark
    sweet cherries, drained
¾ cup port wine

2 tablespoons butter or
    margarine
¼ cup minced onion
3 tablespoons flour
3 tablespoons currant jelly
1 teaspoon bottled sauce for
    gravy

1

About 3 hours before serving: Preheat oven to 325° F. Sprinkle duckling quarters with ½ teaspoon salt. In shallow roasting pan, on rack, roast duckling 2½ to 3 hours or until tender and crisp.

2

Meanwhile, simmer giblets (omitting liver) and neck with 2 cups water, covered, about 1½ hours. Also let cherries stand in ¼ cup of the port wine.

3

When done, remove duckling from roasting pan; place on serving platter. Pour fat from pan. In pan, melt 2 tablespoons butter, stirring to dissolve browned bits in pan. Add onion; cook, stirring, until tender; remove from heat; stir in flour, ½ teaspoon salt, currant jelly, meat sauce, 1½ cups strained giblet broth, ½ cup wine. Cook over medium heat, stirring, until thickened; combine with cherries in wine; heat. Serve duckling on wild rice, if desired. Pour some sauce over duckling; pass rest. Makes 4 servings.

PURPLE-PLUM DUCKLINGS

2 5-pound ducklings, quartered	concentrate, undiluted
onion salt	⅓ cup chili sauce
garlic salt	¼ cup soy sauce
4 oranges, halved crosswise	1 teaspoon Worcestershire
¼ cup butter or margarine	1 teaspoon ginger
1 medium onion, chopped	2 teaspoons prepared mustard
1 17-ounce can purple plums	2 drops hot pepper sauce
1 6-ounce can frozen lemonade	

1

About 3 hours before serving: Sprinkle duckling quarters with onion and garlic salts; set each on orange half and set duckling quarters and orange halves on trivet in roasting pan. Roast at 350° F. for 1½ hours.

2

While ducklings roast, melt butter in large skillet; add onion and cook until tender. Set aside. Empty plums and juice into food mill or strainer set over bowl. Pit and puree plums. Add puree to chopped onion; blend in lemonade and next 6 ingredients; simmer 15 minutes.

3

Remove ducklings, oranges and trivet from roasting pan. Drain off fat. Arrange ducklings and oranges, side by side, in roasting pan; brush with plum sauce and return to 350° F. oven for 15 minutes. Continue roasting and basting with more sauce every 10 minutes until tender and glazed (about 1 hour). Arrange duckling quarters and orange halves on large heated platter; pass rest of sauce. Makes 4 generous servings.

TURKETTI

1¼ cups 2-inch spaghetti pieces
2 cups cooked or canned turkey or chicken, in 1-inch chunks
½ cup diced, cooked ham
¼ cup minced canned pimiento
¼ cup minced green pepper
1 10½-ounce can condensed cream-of-mushroom soup

½ cup turkey or canned chicken broth
⅛ teaspoon celery salt
⅛ teaspoon pepper
½ grated small onion
1½ cups shredded sharp Cheddar cheese (6 ounces)

1

Day before or early in day: Cook spaghetti as label directs; drain. Combine with rest of ingredients except ½ cup of the cheese. Toss lightly; taste; add more seasonings if needed. Pour into 1½-quart casserole. Sprinkle with cheese. Chill.

2

About 1 hour before dinner: Preheat oven to 350° F. Bake casserole, uncovered, 45 minutes or until bubbling hot. Makes 4 servings.

Slices of turkey on hot toast, topped with a mustard-cheese sauce, bacon and tomato—so good it pays to make sure the holiday bird has leftovers

DELMONICO TURKEY SANDWICHES

3 tablespoons butter or margarine
3 tablespoons flour
¾ teaspoon salt
¼ teaspoon prepared mustard
dash cayenne pepper
2 cups milk

½ pound process sharp Cheddar cheese, shredded (2 cups)
4 toast slices
8 medium slices cooked turkey
dash paprika
4 crisp bacon slices
2 medium tomatoes, sliced

1

About 20 minutes before serving: Preheat oven to 450° F. In saucepan over low heat, melt butter. Gradually add flour, salt, mustard, cayenne and milk. Cook, stirring, until thickened. Remove from heat. Stir in cheese until melted. In 10″ by 6″ by 2″ baking dish, arrange toast; top with turkey; pour on cheese sauce; sprinkle with paprika. Bake 10 minutes. Garnish with bacon and tomato slices. Makes 4 servings.

The most popular dishes of all are usually simple ones, like a really marvelous recipe for macaroni and cheese. This one has three quick variations

BAKED MACARONI AND CHEESE

1 small onion, minced	2 cups milk
butter or margarine	½ pound process Cheddar cheese
1 tablespoon flour	½ pound macaroni, in 2½-inch
¼ teaspoon dry mustard	pieces, or elbow macaroni
¾ teaspoon salt	(about 2 cups)
dash pepper	¾ cup fresh bread crumbs

1

About 45 minutes before serving: Preheat oven to 400° F. Grease 1½-quart casserole.

2

Put onion in double boiler with 2 tablespoons butter. When butter is melted, stir in flour, mustard, salt, pepper. Slowly stir in milk; cook until smooth and thickened, stirring often. Slice about three fourths of cheese right into sauce; stir until cheese is melted. (If preferred, grate cheese ahead, using medium grater, or slice it.)

3

Meanwhile, cook macaroni as label directs; drain; turn into casserole. Pour cheese sauce over macaroni, tossing lightly with fork so that all macaroni gets nicely coated. Top with rest of cheese, shredded.

4

Toss bread crumbs with 4 teaspoons melted butter. Sprinkle over cheese. Bake, uncovered, 20 minutes. Makes 4 servings as main dish, or 6 servings when served instead of potatoes. Nice with crisp bacon and broiled tomato halves.

BAKED-TOMATO MACARONI: Arrange 2 or 3 sliced, peeled tomatoes in layers with macaroni and sauce.

BAKED MACARONI WITH GREEN BEANS: In step 2, with cheese, add 2 cups cooked green beans.

BAKED MACARONI WITH HAM: In step 3, with sauce, add ½ to 1½ cups slivered, cooked ham, tongue, chicken or luncheon meat. (If tongue or ham, reduce salt to ½ teaspoon.)

EGGS BENEDICT

A n egg is an egg is an egg—
except when it's an adventure. As here, where it's teamed
with ham and hollandaise sauce for brunch, lunch or supper

EGGS BENEDICT

Hollandaise Sauce, page 80
8 eggs
butter or margarine
8 thin, boiled ham slices, about

6" by 4"
4 English muffins, split, toasted
and buttered
8 parsley sprigs for garnish

1

About 30 minutes before serving: Make Hollandaise Sauce; place container of sauce in pan of hot water to warm up.

2

Meanwhile, poach eggs: Butter skillet. Pour in enough water to cover eggs—about 2 inches. Bring to boil; lower heat so water is just simmering. Break each egg into cup; quickly slip egg into water; repeat with several eggs; cook, covered, to desired doneness (about 3 to 4 minutes). Remove with slotted spoon or pancake turner; keep warm while poaching rest of eggs. Preheat broiler if manufacturer directs.

Broil ham slices 3 minutes or until hot or curled. Fold slices in half; place one on each muffin half; top with poached egg; spoon on hollandaise; garnish with parsley. Makes 8 servings.

irst published in 1930, this recipe has remained a favorite. It's good, easy, economical

BAKED EGGS WITH CHEESE SAUCE

2 tablespoons butter or
  margarine
2 tablespoons flour
dash pepper
½ teaspoon salt

1 teaspoon prepared mustard
1 cup milk
¼ pound process Cheddar cheese,
  shredded (1 cup)
6 eggs

1

About 30 minutes before serving: Melt butter in double boiler; stir in flour, pepper, salt and mustard until smooth, then stir in milk. Cook over boiling water, stirring, until smooth and thickened. Add cheese; stir till melted. Preheat oven to 325° F. Spoon half of cheese sauce into greased 10″ by 6″ by 2″ baking dish. Break eggs, one by one; place on cheese sauce. Cover with rest of sauce. Bake 20 minutes or until eggs are done. Makes 6 servings.

CHIVE-CHEESE SCRAMBLED EGGS

6 eggs
½ teaspoon salt
⅛ teaspoon pepper
6 tablespoons milk

2 3-ounce packages chive cream
  cheese, broken up
2 tablespoons butter or margarine

1

In medium bowl blend eggs with salt, pepper, milk and cheese.

2

In 9-inch skillet, melt butter, tilting skillet to coat bottom and sides. When hot enough to make drop of water sizzle, pour in egg mixture; reduce heat. Cook slowly, gently lifting from bottom with spoon as mixture sets. Cook until set but still moist. Makes 3 or 4 servings.

I f there's any fare more spectacular than a soufflé, it's hard to think of. This one combines cheese and rice for a dish that will stick to your ribs

CHEESE-AND-RICE SOUFFLÉ

2 tablespoons butter or
  margarine
3 tablespoons flour
¾ cup milk
½ pound process sharp

Cheddar cheese
4 eggs
½ teaspoon salt
dash cayenne pepper
1 cup cooked rice

1

About 1 hour before serving: Preheat oven to 325° F. In double boiler, melt butter; stir in flour till smooth, then milk. Cook, stirring, until smooth and thickened. Slice cheese thinly, right into sauce; cook, stirring occasionally, until cheese is melted and sauce is smooth and thickened.

2

Separate eggs, placing whites in large bowl, yolks in small one. To egg yolks, add salt and cayenne; beat with fork; slowly add to cheese sauce, stirring constantly. Remove sauce from heat; fold in rice; set aside.

3

With electric mixer or rotary beater, beat whites until stiff but not dry. Gently fold in cheese-rice mixture. Turn into a 1½-quart greased casserole.

4

Form crown with spoon, by making shallow path in cheese-rice mixture about 1-inch in from edge all the way around. Bake, uncovered, 40 minutes.

5

Serve at once. If dinner is delayed a bit, leave in oven with heat turned down to 250° F., just a few minutes. Make 5 servings.

VEGETABLE STYLE: Just before folding in egg whites, add 1 cup chopped, cooked broccoli or cooked green beans.

breads & coffeecakes

In our opinion, nothing on this earth smells—or tastes—more delicious than bread that is fresh from the oven. These are our very best bakings of all

A sextet of deliciously different hot breads that all start with the store-bought kind

---
QUICK HOT BREADS

FRANKFURTER ROLLS: Preheat oven to 425° F. Use whole frankfurter rolls. Slash each roll into 5 diagonal slices, part-way through. Butter slashes; insert half slice of Cheddar cheese and thin slice of onion in each. Place on cookie sheet. Bake 10 minutes or until cheese melts; sprinkle with chopped parsley.

FRANKFURTER BREAD STICKS: Preheat broiler if manufacturer directs. Slice each half of frankfurter roll lengthwise into two "bread sticks." Brush all over with salad oil or melted butter or margarine. Sprinkle with caraway, poppy or celery seed, or shake in some garlic, celery or onion salt.

CORN MUFFINS: Split corn muffins; butter cut surfaces; top with one of these: chopped walnuts, pecans or almonds, shredded Cheddar or Swiss cheese, then broil until crisp.

CORN TOASTIES: Split each corn toastie into two layers; place on cookie sheet. Spread cut surfaces with softened butter or margarine, then sprinkle with chili powder, poppy seeds, garlic salt or curry powder; toast under broiler.

ENGLISH MUFFINS: Split English muffin by pulling apart; spread cut surface with soft butter or margarine; top with one of these: caraway, sesame or poppy seed, shredded Cheddar or Swiss cheese, then toast in broiler.

BUTTERFLAKE ROLLS: Partly separate "leaves" of each butterflake roll; spread leaves with one of these fillings: pimiento cream cheese, softened with milk, plus chopped, stuffed olives; or mayonnaise mixed with grated Parmesan. Bake at 425° F. 4 to 5 minutes.

OUR GIANT POPOVERS

T ruly huge, yet with an airy interior, crisp and crunchy outside, this is the bread we are most often asked to serve at Good Housekeeping luncheons

---

OUR GIANT POPOVERS

---

6 eggs
2 cups milk
6 tablespoons melted butter
   or margarine

2 cups instant or sifted all-purpose
   flour
1 teaspoon salt

1

About 1 hour 20 minutes before serving: Preheat oven to 375° F. Butter well eight 6-ounce pottery custard cups;* arrange cups on jelly-roll pan or roasting pan.

* We use 6-ounce pottery Chefsware No. 142 custard cups. They may be purchased from Bridge Company, 212 East 52nd Street, New York City 10021.

With electric mixer at low speed, or with hand beater, beat eggs slightly; add milk and melted butter; beat until blended, then gradually beat in flour and salt. Pour batter into custard cups to within ¼ inch of top; wipe off any spills.

Bake popovers 60 minutes, then remove from oven. Quickly cut slit in side of each to let out steam; return them to the oven for 10 to 15 minutes or until their tops are very firm, crisp, deep brown. Then, so bottoms of popovers won't steam and soften, promptly lift them out of custard cups onto rack; or, if necessary, first loosen them with spatula. Serve piping hot, with butter and marmalade or jelly. Makes 8.

PECAN POPOVERS: Make as above. Just before baking, sprinkle 1 tablespoon coarsely chopped pecans over batter in each cup (½ cup in all).

FAMILY POPOVERS: Make up half of recipe for Our Giant Popovers. Butter well nine 3-inch muffin-pan cups. Divide batter among the muffin-pan cups. Bake 40 minutes, then slit and continue as above. Makes 9 popovers.

A real cook can perform miracles. Like turning plain bread into crusty, taste-tempting rolls

TOASTED ROLLS IN LOAF

1 1-pound loaf unsliced white bread
½ cup butter or margarine, softened
½ teaspoon celery seed
¼ teaspoon salt
¼ teaspoon paprika
dash cayenne

1

Preheat oven to 400° F. Trim crusts from top and sides of loaf. (For rounded top, peel off top crust.) Cut almost through to bottom crust of loaf either in 1-inch crosswise slices or diagonally to form diamonds.

2

Mix butter with rest of ingredients; spread on cut surfaces, top and sides of loaf. Place on shallow pan and bake 18 minutes or until golden. Cut apart to serve. Makes about 10 servings.

P

aper-thin, crisp, and ragged at the edges, these keep for up to two weeks without losing a bit of flavor. Before serving, brush with melted butter

---

CORN CRISPS

---

1 cup yellow cornmeal
½ cup sifted all-purpose flour
½ teaspoon salt
¼ teaspoon baking soda

3 tablespoons salad oil
⅓ cup milk
melted butter or margarine

1

Make 2 weeks ahead, or early in day: Preheat oven to 350° F. Sift cornmeal with flour, salt, soda; stir in salad oil, milk. On lightly floured surface, knead dough 8 times or until it holds together.

2

Break off nickel-size piece; with stockinette-covered rolling pin, roll into paper-thin, 5-inch circle with ragged edges. Lay on ungreased cookie sheet. Repeat until all dough is rolled out. Bake 10 minutes or until golden; cool on racks. If for later use (up to 2 weeks), store, covered, in dry place at room temperature.

3

Just before serving, brush each Corn Crisp with melted butter or margarine; sprinkle with salt. Makes 20 to 24.

To vary: Sprinkle celery or poppy seed on Crisps after they're buttered.

SAVORY GARLIC FRENCH BREAD

---

1 36-inch loaf French bread
1 garlic clove
½ cup butter or margarine,

softened
grated Parmesan cheese

1

Preheat oven to 375° F. Slash loaf of bread into diagonal slices, almost to bottom crust. Rub garlic lightly over crust.

2

Mash garlic; combine with butter; spread over cut surfaces of loaf; wrap loaf in aluminum foil, leaving foil partially open at top. Sprinkle cheese over top of loaf. Bake 15 to 20 minutes. Makes about 12 servings.

There's a trick to keeping the berries distributed through the batter—stir them in quickly and bake the muffins at once. These have sugary, crisp tops

BLUEBERRY MUFFINS

1 cup fresh blueberries
granulated sugar
2 cups all-purpose flour
3 teaspoons double-acting baking
    powder

1 teaspoon salt
1 egg
1 cup milk
6 tablespoons salad oil

1

Wash and drain berries; pat dry on paper towels. In bowl, sweeten to taste with 2 or 3 tablespoons sugar; set aside. (Or use 1 cup frozen blueberries; don't sweeten.)

2

Preheat oven to 425° F. Grease twelve 3-inch or fourteen 2½-inch muffin-pan cups well. Into mixing bowl, sift flour, baking powder, salt, 2 tablespoons sugar.

3

Beat egg till frothy; add milk and shortening, mix well. Make small well in center of flour mixture; pour in milk mixture all at once. Stir quickly and lightly—don't beat—until just mixed, but still lumpy. Quickly stir in berries.

4

Quickly fill muffin cups two-thirds full with batter; wipe off any spilled drops. (If batter does not fill all cups, fill empty ones with water to keep grease from burning.) Sprinkle 4 teaspoons granulated sugar over tops of muffins. Bake 25 minutes or until cake tester inserted in center of muffin comes out clean. Run spatula around each muffin to loosen it; lift out into napkin-lined basket and serve piping hot. Makes 12 to 14.

Note: If muffins are done before rest of meal, loosen, then tip slightly in pans and keep warm right in pans so they won't steam and soften. Freeze leftovers for another day.

For 6 muffins: Use 1 egg; halve rest of ingredients. Spoon into six 3-inch muffin-pan cups. Bake as above.

CLARA'S SPECIAL COFFEECAKE

P

erhaps it's the cocoa-and-nut filling. Or maybe it's the sour-cream batter. Whatever the reason, we get lots of requests for Clara's cake

CLARA'S SPECIAL COFFEECAKE

1½ cups granulated sugar	3 eggs
½ cup chopped walnuts	3 cups sifted all-purpose flour
1 tablespoon cocoa	1 tablespoon double-acting
1 teaspoon cinnamon	baking powder
½ cup butter or margarine,	1 teaspoon baking soda
softened	1¼ cups sour cream

1

Early in day: Preheat oven to 375° F. Make filling. In small bowl, combine ½ cup of the sugar, walnuts, cocoa and cinnamon; set aside.

2

In large bowl, with electric mixer at medium speed, cream butter until light and fluffy. Gradually beat in 1 cup sugar. Add eggs, one at a time, beating well after each addition. Sift flour with baking powder and baking soda; beat into egg mixture alternately with sour cream.

Into greased 9-inch tube pan (or 7-cup mold dusted with packaged bread crumbs), pour half of batter (about 2⅓ cups); top with filling; spread remaining batter evenly over filling. Bake 1 hour or until cake tester inserted in center comes out clean. Cool cake completely in pan before removing. Makes 10 servings.

A raisin-studded loaf that is as light as the lilt of a brogue and as sweet as its blarney

IRISH SODA BREAD

4 cups sifted all-purpose flour
¼ cup granulated sugar
1 teaspoon salt
1 teaspoon double-acting baking powder
2 tablespoons caraway seed (optional)

¼ cup butter or margarine
2 cups golden or dark raisins
1⅓ cups buttermilk
1 egg
1 teaspoon baking soda
1 egg yolk, slightly beaten, or a little cream

1

Early in day: Preheat oven to 375° F. Grease 2-quart casserole. Into mixing bowl, sift flour, sugar, salt, baking powder; stir in caraway seed. With pastry blender or 2 knives used scissor-fashion, cut in butter until like coarse cornmeal; stir in raisins. Combine buttermilk, egg, soda; stir into flour mixture until just moistened.

2

Turn dough onto lightly floured surface; knead lightly until smooth; shape into ball. Place in casserole. With sharp knife, make 4-inch cross, ¼-inch deep, in top center. Brush with yolk. Bake 1 hour 10 minutes or until cake tester inserted in center comes out clean. Cool in casserole 10 minutes; remove. Cool before slicing into pie-shaped wedges. Makes 10 to 12 servings.

FRUITED SODA BREAD: Along with raisins, stir in ½ cup halved, candied cherries and ¼ cup diced, preserved orange peel.

STEAMED BOSTON BROWN BREAD

1 cup unsifted whole wheat
 flour
1 cup unsifted rye flour
1 cup yellow cornmeal

1½ teaspoon baking soda
1½ teaspoons salt
¾ cup molasses
2 cups buttermilk

1

About 4 hours before serving: Grease and flour 2-quart mold. Combine flours, cornmeal, soda, salt. Stir in molasses, buttermilk. Turn into mold; cover tightly.

2

Place on trivet in deep kettle. Add enough boiling water to kettle to come half way up sides of mold; cover. Steam 3½ hours or until done, checking water from time to time. Remove from kettle, then unmold onto cake rack.

3

Serve hot with baked beans, boiled tongue, franks, etc. Makes 1 loaf.

Toasted: Butter slices of leftover brown bread; toast under broiler until piping hot.

Raisin: To flour mixture, add 1 cup seeded raisins.

More of a cornmeal custard than a bread, this Southern treat is delicious with lots of butter

MARJIE'S FLUFFY SPOON BREAD

1 quart milk
1 cup cornmeal (yellow or
 white)

1½ teaspoons salt
2 tablespoons butter or margarine
4 eggs

1

About 1 hour and 15 minutes before serving: In double boiler, heat milk; gradually stir in cornmeal mixed with salt; cook, stirring, until smooth and thick. Cover; cook until mushy.

Preheat oven to 425° F. Remove the mush from heat; add butter. In bowl, beat eggs till well blended; slowly stir into mush. Pour into well-greased 1½-quart casserole. Bake, uncovered, 50 to 55 minutes.

3

Serve from casserole, spooning some onto each plate. Eat instead of bread, with lots of butter or margarine (use fork or spoon). Makes 4 or 5 servings.

A marvelous bread for any oc-casion, this one is especially nice for holidays. Because it freezes so well, it can be made well ahead of time, reheated

CRANBERRY-WALNUT BREAD

2 cups sifted all-purpose flour
1 teaspoon baking soda
1 teaspoon salt
¾ cup granulated sugar
1 egg
⅓ cup orange juice
1 teaspoon grated orange peel

3 tablespoons white vinegar plus water to make ⅔ cup liquid
¼ cup melted shortening
1 cup halved or coarsely chopped raw cranberries
1 cup chopped walnuts

1

Day before serving: Preheat oven to 350° F. Grease 9″ by 5″ by 3″ loaf pan. In mixing bowl, sift flour, soda, salt, sugar. With fork, beat egg; stir in orange juice, peel, vinegar-water mixture, shortening. Add, all at once, to flour mixture; stir just until all flour is moistened. Add cran-berries and walnuts; turn into pan.

2

Bake 60 minutes or until cake tester inserted in center comes out clean. Cool in pan 10 minutes; remove; cool; wrap in foil; store overnight before slicing.

Try this bread the next time you make tea sandwiches. Use fluffy cream cheese or orange-flavored butter as sandwich filling.

Note: This bread freezes well too.

W hen they smell this bread baking, its own fragrance mingled with that of chives and garlic and cheese, your family will hardly be able to wait

CHIVE-BUDDED GARLIC BREAD

5½ to 6½ cups all-purpose flour
3 tablespoons granulated sugar
2 teaspoons salt
1 package active dry yeast
½ cup milk
butter or margarine

¼ cup chopped chives
1 teaspoon garlic salt
1 tablespoon grated Parmesan cheese
1 egg yolk, beaten

1

Early in day: In large bowl, combine 2 cups flour, sugar, salt and yeast. In medium saucepan, heat 1½ cups water, milk and 3 tablespoons butter until very warm (120° to 130° F.). Butter does not need to melt. With electric mixer at medium speed, gradually add liquid to flour mixture. Beat 2 minutes, scraping bowl occasionally. Add ¾ cup flour or enough to make thick batter; beat 2 minutes at high speed, scraping bowl occasionally. With wooden spoon, stir in enough additional flour (about 3 cups) to make soft dough.

2

Place dough onto lightly floured surface and knead until smooth and elastic, about 10 minutes. Shape dough into ball and place in large greased bowl; turn once to grease surface. Cover with towel; let rise in warm place (80° to 85° F.), away from draft, 1 hour or until doubled.

3

Punch down dough; turn out onto floured surface; cover with bowl and let rest 15 minutes. Roll dough out ¾ inch thick; cut with 2½-inch biscuit cutter. Melt ½ cup butter; combine with chives, garlic salt and cheese; brush each circle generously on both sides with garlic butter, leaving 4 end pieces unbuttered.

4

On 15½″ by 10½″ by 1″ jelly-roll pan, line circles up to form 2 loaves; cover with towel; let rise in warm place until double in bulk, about 1 hour. Brush with egg yolk.

5

Preheat oven to 400° F. Bake loaves 30 minutes or until golden. Remove from pan immediately and cool on racks. Makes 2 loaves.

CHIVE-BUDDED GARLIC BREAD

Onion-soup mix has many uses, not the least of which is as flavoring for this superb loaf

BRAIDED ONION BREAD

6 to 6½ cups all-purpose flour
1 package active dry yeast
1 envelope onion-soup mix
2 tablespoons granulated sugar
2 teaspoons salt
¼ teaspoon baking soda

2 tablespoons butter or
  margarine
1 cup sour cream
3 eggs, beaten
sesame seed

1

Early in day: In large bowl, combine 2 cups flour, yeast, soup mix, sugar, salt and baking soda.

2

In small saucepan, heat 1 cup water, butter and sour cream until very warm (120° to 130° F.). Butter does not need to melt.

3

With electric mixer at medium speed, add sour cream mixture to flour mixture; beat 2 minutes. Add all but 2 tablespoons of the beaten eggs and enough additional flour (about 2 cups) to make thick batter. With wooden spoon, stir in enough flour (about 2 cups) to make soft dough. Place dough on lightly floured surface and knead until smooth, about 5 minutes. Place in large greased bowl, turning once to grease surface. Cover with towel; let rise in warm place (80° to 85° F.) 1½ hours or until doubled.

4

Punch down dough; turn onto floured surface; cover with bowl and let rest 10 minutes. Divide dough into 6 equal parts. With the palms of your hands, roll 3 of the parts into strips 15 inches long. Braid the 3 strips together, sealing ends. Repeat with remaining 3 parts of dough. Place braids on greased cookie sheet, side by side; cover and let rise in warm place until doubled.

5

Preheat oven to 350° F. Brush braids with remaining 2 tablespoons beaten egg; sprinkle with sesame seed. Bake 40 to 45 minutes or until golden and firm. Cool on racks. Makes 2 onion braids.

Note: This bread freezes well.

Years ago, a bread like this took all day to make. Now easier-to-use, improved active dry yeast cuts the rising time down to little more than two hours

COLOSSAL CORN BREAD

7 to 7½ cups all-purpose flour	2 cups milk
1 package active dry yeast	⅓ cup shortening
⅓ cup granulated sugar	2 eggs, well beaten
1 tablespoon salt	1 cup yellow cornmeal

1

Day before: In large bowl, thoroughly mix 2 cups flour, yeast, sugar and salt.

2

In small saucepan, heat milk, ¼ cup water and shortening until very warm (120° to 130° F.). Shortening does not need to melt.

3

With electric mixer at medium speed, gradually add milk mixture to flour mixture; beat 2 minutes. Add eggs, cornmeal and enough flour (about 1 cup) to make thick batter. Beat at high speed 2 minutes. With wooden spoon, stir in enough flour (3 to 4 cups) to make soft dough.

4

Place on lightly floured surface and knead until smooth, about 5 minutes. Place in large, greased bowl; turn once to grease surface. Cover with towel and let rise in warm place (80° to 85° F.) 1½ hours or until doubled. Grease 9″ by 5″ by 3″ loaf pan.

5

Punch down dough; turn onto floured surface; cover with bowl and let rest 10 minutes. Knead a minute or two; shape into one oval and place, smooth side up, in pan.

6

Cover bread and let rise in warm place until doubled in bulk (about 35 minutes).

7

Meanwhile, preheat oven to 375° F. Bake bread 50 to 60 minutes (top of bread will brown quickly). Turn out on side on rack to cool. Makes 1 loaf.

JAMBOREE COFFEECAKE

S tudded with pockets of rasp-
berry jam baked to melting goodness, and spread with an
almond-flavored glaze, this cake is itself a cause for celebration

JAMBOREE COFFEECAKE

5 to 5½ cups all-purpose flour	1 tablespoon lemon peel
½ cup granulated sugar	1 teaspoon mace
1½ teaspoons salt	2 eggs
2 packages active dry yeast	raspberry jam
1 cup milk	Icing Glaze (opposite)
butter or margarine	

1

Early in day: In large bowl, combine 3 cups flour, sugar, salt and yeast.
In medium saucepan, heat milk, ¼ cup water and ½ cup butter until
very warm (120° to 130° F.). Butter does not have to melt. Remove
from heat; stir in lemon peel and mace.

2

With electric mixer at medium speed, gradually add liquid to flour
mixture. Beat 2 minutes; beat eggs into mixture; add 1 cup flour or

enough to make thick batter; beat 2 minutes; stir in enough flour to make soft dough (about 1½ cups) .

3

Place dough on lightly floured surface and knead until smooth, about 10 minutes; place dough in greased bowl, turn once to grease surface; cover with towel; let rise in warm place (80° to 85° F.) 1½ hours or until doubled in bulk. Meanwhile, grease bottom and sides of 10″ by 2½″ round cake pan.

4

Punch down dough; turn out on lightly floured surface; cover with bowl and let rest 15 minutes. Shape dough into ball; with floured rolling pin, flatten it gently into 8-inch round. Place in cake pan; cover; let rise in warm place until sides of dough are about 1¼ inches below rim of pan, about 1 hour.

5

Preheat oven to 350° F. With floured round handle of wooden spoon, make deep hole in center of dough; with tip of small knife, insert some of the raspberry jam, filling hole from bottom to top of cake. Continue making holes over surface of dough in same manner, about 2 inches apart, flouring handle each time and being sure to fill each hole with jam immediately after making it. Bake 50 to 60 minutes, or until cake tester inserted in center comes out clean. Remove from oven; place on rack. Let cool 10 minutes in pan; remove cake, cool. If necessary fill holes with additional jam. Frost with Icing Glaze. Makes 16 servings.

Note: If desired, cake may be frozen without Icing Glaze, spread with Glaze after defrosting.

ICING GLAZE

1 cup confectioners' sugar   *2 tablespoons warm milk*
¼ teaspoon almond extract

1

In small bowl, combine confectioners' sugar, almond extract and milk until smooth. Spread over cake and around jam holes.

T here's no need to get up before dawn to serve this for breakfast. Make, bake, and freeze it any time. Left to thaw overnight, it will reheat in minutes

ALMOND BRAID

2½ cups all-purpose flour
 1 teaspoon salt
 1 teaspoon nutmeg or mace
 1 package active dry yeast
⅓ cup granulated sugar

½ cup milk
¼ cup butter or margarine
 1 egg, beaten
Orange Icing (below)
blanched almonds, split

1

About 4 hours before serving: In large bowl, thoroughly combine 1 cup flour, salt, nutmeg, yeast and sugar.

2

In small saucepan, combine milk, ¼ cup water and butter; heat until very warm (120° to 130° F.). Butter does not have to melt.

3

With electric mixer at medium speed, gradually add milk mixture to flour mixture; beat 2 minutes, scraping sides of bowl occasionally. Add egg and enough additional flour (about 1 cup) to make a soft dough. Beat at high speed 2 minutes, scraping sides of bowl occasionally. Turn out onto floured surface; knead in remaining flour until dough is smooth and elastic (about 5 minutes). Place in greased bowl; turn once. Cover; let rise in warm place (80 to 85° F.) 1 hour or until doubled.

4

Turn onto floured surface; cover with bowl and let rest 10 minutes. Knead slightly; divide into 4 parts; shape 3 of them into rolls about 14 inches long; place, on greased baking sheet, 1 inch apart.

5

Braid rolls loosely, sealing ends together. Shape fourth piece of dough into 3 rolls, each 12 inches long; braid loosely; place on top of first braid, pinching ends into larger braid. Cover and let rise until doubled, about 45 minutes. Meanwhile, preheat oven to 350° F. Bake 20 minutes or until done. Remove from baking sheet; cool on rack; frost.

ORANGE ICING: In small bowl, over hot water, heat 1 tablespoon butter, 1 teaspoon grated orange peel, 1 tablespoon each orange juice and lemon juice until butter is melted. Remove from hot water; stir in 1¼ cups sifted confectioners' sugar. Coat braid. Sprinkle with almonds.

A rich, light coffeecake with a creamy nut filling, potica is a welcome gift from Yugoslavia

POTICA

3½ to 3¾ cups all-purpose flour
granulated sugar
salt
  1 package active dry yeast
  1 cup milk
butter or margarine

2 eggs, separated
2 cups ground walnuts
6 tablespoons light cream
½ teaspoon vanilla extract
2 tablespoons fresh bread crumbs

1

Early in day: In large bowl, thoroughly mix 1¼ cups flour, ¼ cup sugar, 1 teaspoon salt and yeast. In small saucepan, heat milk, ¼ cup water and ¼ cup butter until very warm (120° to 130° F.). Butter does not have to melt. With electric mixer at medium speed, gradually beat milk mixture into flour mixture; beat 2 minutes. Add egg yolks and 2 cups flour or enough flour to make thick batter; beat at high speed 2 minutes. With wooden spoon, stir in enough remaining flour to make soft dough.

2

Place on lightly floured surface and knead until smooth. Place dough in greased bowl; turn once to grease surface. Cover and let rise in warm place (80° to 85° F.) 1 hour or until doubled.

3

Meanwhile, in medium bowl, stir walnuts, ⅔ cup sugar, cream, ½ teaspoon salt and vanilla. In small saucepan, melt 2 tablespoons butter; add bread crumbs and cook until golden; add to nut mixture. In medium bowl, with electric mixer at high speed, beat egg whites until stiff; fold into nut mixture.

4

Punch down dough; divide in half. On lightly floured surface, roll one half into 16″ by 9″ rectangle. Spread with half of filling; starting from short end, roll up, jelly-roll fashion; place in one greased 9″ by 5″ by 3″ loaf pan. Repeat with remaining dough and filling.

5

Let loaves rise until almost doubled, 30 to 40 minutes. Preheat oven to 375° F. Bake 35 to 40 minutes or until each sounds hollow when tapped with fingers. Remove from pans to rack to cool. Makes 2 loaves.

S

tollen, the Christmas bread of Germany, has been taken over by all lovers of good things

CHRISTMAS STOLLEN

5 cups all-purpose flour
1 package active dry yeast
½ teaspoon salt
granulated sugar
¼ teaspoon nutmeg
1 cup milk
butter or margarine
2 eggs, beaten

½ cup finely cut citron
½ cup finely cut candied
   cherries
1 cup blanched, slivered
   almonds
grated peel of 1 lemon
1 cup raisins
½ teaspoon cinnamon

1

Early in day: In large bowl, thoroughly mix 2 cups flour, yeast, salt, ½ cup sugar and nutmeg.

2

In small saucepan, heat milk, ¼ cup water and ¾ cup butter until very warm (120° to 130° F.) Butter does not have to melt.

3

With electric mixer at medium speed, gradually beat milk mixture into flour mixture; beat 2 minutes. Add eggs and enough flour (about 1 cup) to make thick batter. Beat at high speed 2 minutes. With wooden spoon, stir in citron and next 4 ingredients and enough remaining flour (about 2 cups) to make soft dough.

4

Place on lightly floured surface and knead until smooth, about 5 minutes. Place in large greased bowl; turn once to grease surface. Cover with towel and let rise in warm place (80° to 85° F.) 1½ hours or until doubled. Meanwhile, grease large cookie sheet.

5

Punch down dough; turn onto floured surface; cover with bowl and let rest 10 minutes. Knead a minute or two, then roll into 18″ by 12″ oval, ½ inch thick. Brush with some of ¼ cup melted butter; sprinkle with combined cinnamon and 2 tablespoons sugar.

6

Make lengthwise crease down center of dough; fold over. Remove to cookie sheet. Push into shape of crescent; with palm of hand, press down along crease to shape. Brush with rest of melted butter, then let rise until nearly doubled (about 1 hour).

7

Meanwhile, preheat oven to 350° F. When ready, bake bread 50 minutes or until golden. Cool, then sprinkle with sifted confectioners' sugar. Store tightly covered, or freeze. It keeps well. Makes 1 stollen.

A loaf as tall as a chef's hat, with a melt-in-your-mouth consistency and a lemon-mace tang

---

LEMON BUBBLE LOAF

---

granulated sugar
1/4 teaspoon mace
grated peel of 2 lemons
  5 to 6 cups all-purpose flour
  1 teaspoon salt

3 packages active dry yeast
1 cup milk
butter or margarine
2 eggs, well beaten

1

Early in day: In small bowl, combine 1/2 cup sugar, mace, lemon peel; set aside. In large bowl, combine 2 cups flour, salt, yeast and 1/2 cup sugar. In small saucepan, combine milk, 1/2 cup water and 1/4 cup butter; heat until very warm (120° to 130° F). Butter does not have to melt. Gradually beat milk mixture into flour mixture; beat 2 minutes, scraping sides of bowl. Add eggs and enough additional flour to make soft dough (about 1 cup). Beat 2 minutes; stir in remaining flour. On smooth surface, sprinkle half of remaining flour; turn dough onto it and knead until smooth and elastic with small blisters under surface (about 5 minutes). Place dough in large greased bowl; turn once to grease surface. Cover with towel; let rise in warm place (80° to 85° F.) about 45 minutes or until doubled; punch down.

2

Turn dough onto floured surface; cover with bowl; let rest 10 minutes. Meanwhile, grease 16″ by 4″ by 4″ angel-loaf pan, or use two 9″ by 5″ by 3″ loaf pans. Cut dough in half; cut each half into 16 equal pieces. Shape 16 pieces into balls, tucking ends under; place these in layer in pan, brushing with 1 tablespoon melted butter; sprinkle with half of lemon mixture. Shape rest of pieces; arrange as second layer, brushing and sprinkling as before. Let rise, covered, in warm place, 45 minutes or until doubled. Preheat oven to 350° F. Bake 35 minutes or until done; cool in pan 5 minutes, then cool on rack. Bake smaller loaves 30 minutes.

Master this single recipe
and you will have the basis for dozens of delectable breads

BASIC SWEET DOUGH

---

8 cups all-purpose flour
1 cup granulated sugar
1 teaspoon salt
2 packages active dry yeast
½ teaspoon ground cardamom,

or 1½ tablespoons grated
lemon peel
1½ cups milk
1 cup butter or margarine
2 eggs

1

Early in day: In large bowl, combine 2 cups flour, granulated sugar, salt, yeast and cardamom.

2

In medium saucepan, heat milk with ½ cup water and butter until very warm (120° to 130° F.). Butter does not have to melt. Gradually add milk mixture to flour mixture; with electric mixer at medium speed, beat 2 minutes. Beat in eggs and gradually add 3 cups of flour; beat 2 minutes at medium speed or until a soft dough. With wooden spoon, gradually beat in remaining 3 cups of flour; turn onto lightly floured surface; knead until smooth and elastic.

3

Place dough in greased bowl; turn over to grease surface; cover with towel; let rise in warm place (80° to 85° F.) 1 hour or until doubled. Punch down dough. Use all or half of it, as each of our yeast-bread recipes, which follow, directs you.

RAISIN LOAF: At the end of step 2 in Basic Dough, knead in ¾ cup raisins and ⅓ cup sliced blanched almonds; complete as in step 3. Divide punched down dough into 3 pieces. With palms of hands, roll each piece into 22-inch lengths; braid 3 rolls together; pinch ends together. Grease well 9-inch springform pan; wind braid around and around, making a coil that covers bottom of pan. Let rise again until almost doubled. Preheat oven to 350° F. Brush dough with beaten egg, and sprinkle with ¼ cup sliced blanched almonds. Bake 1 hour and 15 minutes or until bread sounds hollow when tapped with fingers. Cool in pan 10 minutes; turn out on rack; cool. Makes 1 loaf.

RAISIN LOAF
FRUITED FROSTED BRAID
ALMOND DESSERT CAKE
BRAIDED ROLLS

BRAIDED ROLLS

Early in day: Use half Basic Sweet Dough, page 111. On floured surface, cut raised dough into 12 pieces. Cut one of pieces into thirds; with hands, roll each third into 10-inch rope. Now braid these 3 ropes into one; tuck ends under; place on greased cookie sheet. Roll and braid other 11 pieces of dough in same way, arranging them on cookie sheet. Let rolls rise in warm place (80° to 85° F.) until almost doubled. Meanwhile, preheat oven to 350° F. Brush rolls with beaten egg, then bake 15 minutes or until golden. Makes 12 rolls.

KNOTTED ROLLS: Cut raised dough in half. Roll out one half at a time into a 12″ by 8″ rectangle; cut into strips 8″ by 1½″. Loosely tie each strip into a knot. Place on greased cookie sheet. Let rise in warm place (80° F. to 85° F.) until almost doubled, then preheat oven to 350° F. Brush raised rolls with beaten egg. Bake 15 minutes or until golden. Makes 16 rolls.

Our basic sweet dough (page 111) , baked, split, and filled with creamy pudding, topped with a honey glaze, split almonds, and one gorgeous candied cherry

ALMOND DESSERT CAKE (pictured on page 110)

half Basic Sweet Dough, page 111
1 egg yolk, slightly beaten
1 3¼-ounce package regular vanilla pudding-and-pie-filling mix
¼ teaspoon almond extract
½ cup heavy or whipping cream,

whipped
1 tablespoon granulated sugar
3 tablespoons honey
1 tablespoon butter or margarine
1 candied cherry for garnish
about 1 tablespoon blanched, sliced almonds for garnish

1

Early in day: On lightly floured surface, knead raised dough a few times to form smooth ball. Place in greased 9-inch layer-cake pan. Push dough out to cover pan. Cover with towel; let rise in warm place (80° to 85° F.) until doubled—about 1 hour.

2

Preheat oven to 350° F. Brush top of dough with beaten egg yolk. Bake 35 to 40 minutes or until sides of cake sound hollow when tapped.

(Peek after 20 minutes; if too brown, cover lightly with foil.) When done, cool in pan, on rack, 10 minutes; with broad spatula, loosen from pan; invert on rack, and lift off pan. Cool cake, right side up .

3

In small saucepan, prepare vanilla filling as label directs but reduce milk to 1 cup. Remove from heat; lay waxed paper directly on top of filling; refrigerate until just cool; then fold in extract and cream. Split cooled cake into two layers. Spread filling on bottom layer, then cover with top layer.

4

In small saucepan, combine sugar, honey and butter; bring to a boil; remove from heat. With mixture, quickly glaze top of cake. Garnish with candied cherry and sliced almonds. Chill about 2 hours before serving. Makes 8 to 10 wedges.

H

ere strips of sweet dough are filled with fruit, then braided together, baked and glazed

---

FRUITED FROSTED BRAID (pictured on page 110)

1 cup golden raisins
¾ cup diced candied orange peel
¼ cup diced citron
all-purpose flour

half Basic Sweet Dough, page 111
1 egg yolk, slightly beaten
½ cup confectioners' sugar

1

Early in day: In bowl, toss raisins, diced orange peel and citron with bit of flour; set aside.

2

Turn raised dough onto lightly floured surface and knead a few minutes until smooth; then cut into 3 even pieces. On floured surface, with floured, stockinette-covered rolling pin, roll each piece of dough into strip about 12″ by 4″, making 3 strips in all. Spread one-third of floured fruit down lengthwise center of one of these strips; brush edges with egg yolk. Bring edges together, forming roll; seal edges. Repeat with other 2 strips. Then braid these 3 filled rolls together, tucking ends under; place on large greased cookie sheet. Let rise, covered, in warm place (80° to 85° F.) till almost doubled.

3

Preheat oven to 350° F. Brush raised braid with egg yolk. Bake 35 minutes or until golden; cool on rack. Now mix sugar with 1 tablespoon water; brush over braid. Makes 1 braid.

BUNCHED SUGAR BUNS

A breakfast treat that can be made the day before from hot-roll mix, reheated for serving

BUNCHED SUGAR BUNS

1 13¾-ounce package hot-roll mix	grated peel of 2 lemons
½ cup butter or margarine, softened	1½ teaspoon ground cinnamon
	1 teaspoon mace
¾ cup packed light brown sugar	3 tablespoons granulated sugar
	dash cream of tartar

1

Day before serving: Make hot-roll mix as label directs. Let rise once; punch down.

2

On floured surface, with stockinette-covered rolling pin, roll out dough into 24″ by 18″ rectangle.

3

Spread butter evenly over dough; sprinkle with mixture of brown sugar, lemon peel, cinnamon and mace. Starting with long edge, roll dough up tightly, jelly-roll fashion. Then cut roll crosswise into 25 1-inch-wide slices; place, cut side up, close together, in greased 8″ by 8″ by 2″ cake pan. Let rise again till almost doubled—about 45 minutes.

4

Meanwhile, preheat oven to 375° F. Bake buns 35 minutes or until done, covering top with foil if they get too brown. Let buns stand in pan, on rack. In saucepan, boil together granulated sugar, ½ cup water and cream of tartar until it starts to turn a caramel color. Remove buns from pan; brush tops with this sugar glaze. Cool completely on rack. Wrap tightly in foil; store overnight.

5

20 minutes before serving: Preheat oven to 300° F. Heat foil-wrapped buns, 15 minutes or until heated through. Makes 25 pull-apart buns.

hoever Sally Lunn was, she had a light hand with yeast bread, as her specialty shows

SALLY LUNN

3½ to 4 cups all-purpose flour	*1 cup milk*
3 tablespoons granulated sugar	*3 tablespoons butter or margarine*
1¼ teaspoons salt	*2 eggs*
1 package active dry yeast	

1

About 3½ hours before serving: In large bowl, thoroughly mix 1¼ cups flour, granulated sugar, salt and yeast.

2

In small saucepan, combine milk and butter; heat until very warm (120° to 130° F.). Butter does not have to melt. With electric mixer at medium speed, gradually beat milk into flour mixture, then beat 2 minutes. Add eggs and 1 cup flour. Beat at high speed 2 minutes, scraping sides of bowl occasionally. Stir in 1½ cups flour or enough to make thick batter. Cover and let rise in warm place (80° to 85° F.) until doubled—about 1 hour.

3

Stir batter down and beat very well. Pour into well-greased and floured 9-inch tube pan. Cover and let rise in warm place (80° to 85° F.) until doubled—about 1 hour.

4

Preheat oven to 300° F. Bake 1 hour or until golden brown. With spatula, loosen sides; cool on rack before slicing. Makes 1 loaf.

EMILIE'S CHOCOLATE-FILLED DOUGHNUTS

8¼ cups all-purpose flour
granulated sugar
  1 teaspoon salt
  1 package active dry yeast
  ¾ cup butter or margarine
  2 cups milk
  3 egg yolks, beaten

  1 egg
  ¼ cup sour cream
  1 6-ounce package semisweet-
    chocolate pieces
  6 tablespoons light cream
  3 egg whites, slightly beaten
shortening or salad oil

1

About 3 hours before serving: In large bowl, thoroughly mix 6 cups flour, ¾ cup sugar, salt and yeast.

2

In medium saucepan, heat ⅓ cup water, butter and milk, until very warm (120° to 130° F.). Butter does not have to melt.

3

With electric mixer at medium speed, gradually add milk mixture to flour mixture. Beat 2 minutes, scraping bowl occasionally. Add egg yolks, 1 egg and sour cream and beat at medium speed for 5 minutes. Stir in enough additional flour to make soft dough (about 2¼ cups).

4

Turn dough onto floured surface; knead until smooth and elastic, about 5 minutes. Shape dough into ball and place in large greased bowl, turning once to grease surface. Cover with towel; let rise in warm place (80° to 85° F.), away from drafts, until doubled, about 1 hour.

Meanwhile, in saucepan over low heat, melt chocolate pieces with light cream, stirring until smooth. Cool.

5

On floured surface, roll dough ½ inch thick. Cut with floured 2-inch cookie cutter. Place ½ teaspoon chocolate mixture in center of half of circles. Brush edges of these circles with slightly beaten egg whites. Top with rest of circles; pinch edges together firmly. Arrange on floured cookie sheets; cover with clean towel; let rise in warm place (80° to 85° F.) until almost doubled and light to the touch.

6

To fry: In deep saucepan, put enough shortening or salad oil to come halfway up side. Heat to 375° F. on deep-fat thermometer. Fry doughnuts, a few at a time, until golden brown and done, turning once. Lift out with slotted spoon; hold over pan a few seconds. Drain on crumpled paper towels. Roll in sugar. Makes about 3½ dozen.

In France, brioches are seldom absent from the breakfast table. No wonder—they're so good!

BERT'S BRIOCHES

2¼ to 2½ cups all-purpose flour
¼ cup granulated sugar
¼ teaspoon salt
1 package active dry yeast
¼ cup milk

⅓ cup butter or margarine
1 egg
2 egg yolks
½ teaspoon lemon extract
salad oil

1

Day before: In large bowl, combine 1 cup flour, sugar, salt and yeast. In medium saucepan, heat ¼ cup water, milk and butter until very warm (180° to 185° F.). Butter does not have to melt. With electric mixer at medium speed, gradually add liquid to dry ingredients. Beat 2 minutes. Add egg and yolks and lemon extract. Stir in 1 cup flour or enough to make thick batter. With spoon, stir in additional flour to make stiff batter. Beat by hand 5 minutes. Brush top of dough with salad oil; cover with towel; let rise in warm place (80° to 85° F.) until doubled, about 1½ hours. Cover with waxed paper and damp towel; refrigerate about 12 hours.

2

Early in day: Grease twelve 2½-inch or 3-inch muffin-pan cups. With floured hands, pinch off enough dough to form 2-inch ball; place ball in muffin-pan cup. Form 1-inch ball; gently press onto larger dough ball; repeat until dough is used up. Brush tops with salad oil. Cover with towel; let rise in warm place until doubled. Preheat oven to 375° F. Bake 15 minutes or until done. Remove from pans; cool on rack. Makes 18 to 20.

BRUNCH BRIOCHES: Turn dough onto lightly floured surface; roll into 14″ by 6″ by ½″ rectangle; cut into 12 lengthwise strips. Braid 3 strips together; cut into thirds; pinch ends together. Repeat with other strips. Set on greased cookie sheet. Cover with towel; let rise in warm place (80° to 85° F.) until doubled, about 1 hour. Meanwhile, preheat oven to 375° F. Bake dough 12 minutes or until done. While brioches are warm, frost with sugar glaze. Makes 12.

SUGAR GLAZE: In small bowl, combine ¾ cup confectioners' sugar, ½ teaspoon vanilla extract and 3 to 4 teaspoons water until smooth and of frosting consistency, adding a few drops more water if needed.

The meringue is baked *inside* this double-ring coffee cake, combining with cinnamon, nuts, raisins and chocolate to produce a many-flavored delight

CHOCOLATE-MERINGUE COFFEE CAKE

2½ cups all-purpose flour
.granulated sugar
  ¼ teaspoon salt
   2 packages active dry yeast
  ½ cup milk
  ½ pound butter or margarine

3 eggs, separated
1 teaspoon cinnamon
½ cup chopped walnuts
¼ cup cut-up raisins
½ cup semisweet-chocolate pieces

1

Day before: In large bowl, thoroughly mix ¾ cup flour, 2 tablespoons sugar, salt and yeast. In small saucepan, heat milk, ¼ cup water and butter until very warm (120° to 130° F.). Butter does not have to melt. With electric mixer at medium speed, gradually beat milk mixture into flour mixture; beat 2 minutes. Add egg yolks and 1¾ cups flour or enough to make smooth dough. Refrigerate along with egg whites.

2

Early in day: Grease 10-inch tube pan. In small bowl, combine cinnamon, 3 tablespoons sugar, walnuts and raisins. Preheat oven to 350° F. In small bowl, with electric mixer at medium speed, beat egg whites to thick fluffy meringue while gradually adding 1 cup sugar. Divide refrigerated dough in half. On lightly floured, cloth-covered surface, roll dough into rectangle 20" by 12". Spread half of meringue over dough; sprinkle with half of walnut mixture and ¼ cup of chocolate.

3

Starting at long side of rectangle, roll up dough jelly-roll fashion until it lies seam side down, lifting cloth as you roll. Bring ends of roll just together in ring. With help of cloth, lift ring into greased pan. Gently fit into tube pan, having ends slightly overlapping.

4

With rest of dough, repeat steps 2 and 3, making second ring. With pan turned so overlapping ends of roll are at your right, lift second roll of dough into greased pan with its overlapping ends to your left.

5

Bake about 1 hour or until golden brown. Cool cake in pan 20 minutes, then remove from pan and cool on rack. Makes 12 servings.

cakes
&
pies

This collection of truly luscious pastries has won the blue ribbon we cherish most—selection by our readers as their favorites of all they have tried

F

or the cook who puts her heart into it—a magnificent eight-layered, chocolate-filled torte that takes three days to make and disappears in just minutes

DOBOS TORTE

1 15- or 16-ounce package angel-food cake mix
few drops yellow food color
1 16-ounce package semisweet-chocolate pieces
1 8-ounce package unsweetened chocolate squares
1½ cups butter or margarine,
softened
2 cups sifted confectioners' sugar
3 egg yolks (or 2 eggs), unbeaten
1 teaspoon instant coffee
⅔ cup granulated sugar
¼ teaspoon cream of tartar

1

3 days ahead: Preheat oven to 350° F. Prepare cake mix as label directs; tint cake batter delicate yellow. Bake in four 8-inch ungreased layer-cake pans, lined with waxed paper, for 25 to 30 minutes. Cool layers, upside down, on racks. Remove from pans. Wrap in foil; chill.

2

2 days ahead: Over hot, *not boiling,* water, melt both chocolates; cool.

3

With electric mixer at medium speed, beat butter until fluffy; add confectioners' sugar gradually, then egg yolks, one at a time, beating until very fluffy; blend in melted chocolate and coffee.

4

Carefully split each cake layer in two, making 8 thin layers. Set aside best layer for top. Set 1 of cake layers on cake plate. With about ⅔ cup frosting, frost it generously; place another layer on top; frost; repeat until all but reserved layer have been used; set it on waxed paper.

5

In small saucepan, combine granulated sugar, ⅓ cup water and cream of tartar. Bring to boil, stirring, then cook, uncovered, *just until golden,* no longer. Stir until bubbles are gone. Quickly spread the caramel glaze over top of reserved layer. Before caramel hardens, with well-buttered silver knife, mark caramel top into 12 wedges—deep marks. Heat kitchen knife in boiling water and retrace marks, right down to cake. Set layer on others; frost sides with chocolate frosting, ending with ½-inch border around edge of caramel. Refrigerate.

6

To serve: With sharp knife, "saw" through markings. Makes 12 servings.

DOBOS TORTE

OLD DOMINION POUNDCAKE

T he "Old Dominion" was Colonial Virginia, whose hospitable ladies served this rich poundcake on every possible occasion, from morning to midnight

OLD DOMINION POUNDCAKE

8 large eggs, separated	2 tablespoons lemon juice
1½ cups butter	2¼ teaspoons vanilla extract
2¼ cups sifted all-purpose flour	⅛ teaspoon salt
¼ teaspoon baking soda	1½ teaspoons cream of tartar
granulated sugar	confectioners' sugar

1

Day before: Let eggs stand at room temperature 1 hour. Butter should be just soft enough to be worked easily. Grease well, then flour a cast-aluminum bundt pan, measuring 10″ by 4½″. Sift together flour, soda and 1¼ cups granulated sugar. Preheat oven to 325° F.

2

In large bowl, with electric mixer at low speed, just barely blend butter with flour mixture, then with lemon juice, vanilla. At low speed, beat in egg yolks, one at a time, just until blended; do not overbeat. Set aside.

In large bowl, with mixer at high speed, beat egg whites until frothy; add salt, then gradually 1 cup granulated sugar with cream of tartar, beating well after each addition. Beat until soft peaks form. Gently fold beaten egg whites into cake batter; turn into prepared pan. With rubber spatula, gently cut through batter once or twice. Bake cake at 325° F. 1½ hours, or until cake tester inserted in center comes out clean. (Do not peek at cake during baking.) Turn off oven heat; let cake remain in oven 15 minutes; remove it to rack to cool 15 minutes longer. Remove cake from pan; cool on rack. Garnish with confectioners' sugar. Makes 12 servings.

Poundcake with a difference— flecks of semisweet chocolate and a scattering of walnuts

WALNUT-CHIP POUNDCAKE

2 cups sifted cake flour	semisweet-chocolate pieces
¼ teaspoon salt	1 cup shortening
1 teaspoon double-acting baking powder	1 cup granulated sugar
	5 eggs, unbeaten
¼ teaspoon mace (optional)	1 teaspon vanilla extract
1 6-ounce package well-chilled	½ cup chopped walnuts

1

Early in day: Preheat oven to 300° F. Grease, then line with waxed paper, 10″ by 5″ by 3″ loaf pan. Sift flour, salt, baking powder, mace. Finely grind chocolate, 3 or 4 pieces at a time, in food chopper.

2

In large bowl, with electric mixer at medium speed, beat shortening with sugar until light and fluffy. Beat in eggs, one at a time, until very creamy—about 8 minutes altogether. At low speed, beat in flour mixture, vanilla, walnuts and chocolate just until smooth. Turn into pan. Bake 1½ hours, or until cake tester inserted in center comes out clean. Cool in pan 10 minutes; remove from pan; cool on rack. Makes 12 servings.

LUXURY LOAF: Use ungreased waxed-paper-lined 10″ by 5″ by 3″ loaf pan. Substitute sifted all-purpose flour for cake flour; increase salt to ½ teaspoon. Add grated rind of 1 orange and ¼ cup orange juice alternately with flour mixture; reduce nuts to ¼ cup. Bake at 300° F. 1 hour 40 minutes, or until done.

Ground orange peel and raisins

go into the batter, then, once that is baked, a luscious almond-orange sauce is spooned all over the top to soak in

---

BUTTERY ORANGE-RAISIN CAKE

---

2 medium oranges
granulated sugar
¼ teaspoon almond extract
2 cups dark raisins
1½ cups milk
2 tablespoons vinegar
1 cup butter or margarine,

softened
4 eggs
4 cups sifted all-purpose flour
2 teaspoons double-acting
  baking powder
2 teaspoons baking soda
½ teaspoon salt

1

Early in day, or day before: Squeeze juice from oranges; strain; reserve peels. In small bowl, place ½ cup granulated sugar and ½ cup orange juice; mix well until sugar is dissolved. Stir in almond extract; refrigerate.

2

Onto waxed paper, using fine blade of food grinder, alternately grind some of reserved orange peels, then some raisins (be careful not to have long "strings" of raisins) ; set aside.

3

Preheat oven to 350° F. Grease 3-quart cast-aluminum bundt pan. Into small bowl, pour milk, then vinegar.

4

In large bowl, with electric mixer at high speed, cream butter; gradually beat in 2 cups granulated sugar. At medium speed, add eggs one at a time, beating well after each addition.

5

Sift flour with baking powder, baking soda and salt. At medium speed, beat into egg mixture alternately with stirred milk mixture, beginning and ending with flour mixture. With rubber spatula, fold in orange-peel-and-raisin mixture, in small amounts, until thoroughly blended. Pour into pan and bake 60 minutes, or until cake tester inserted in center comes out clean. Remove cake from oven; turn off oven.

6

Spoon about 6 tablespoons of reserved orange syrup over top and between cake and sides of pan. Return cake, still in pan, to turned-off oven. Leave cake in oven about 1 hour. With small spatula, loosen cake from pan all around. Invert cake on plate; cool; store covered.

Delicious served warm, with extra syrup as sauce. Makes 12 servings.

PETITE BUTTERY ORANGE-RAISIN CAKE: Halve all ingredients; bake in greased 2-quart mold at 350° F. 45 to 50 minutes. Makes 6 to 8 servings.

The topping bakes on the bottom and then is inverted for all to admire. The taste? Luscious

---

PINEAPPLE UPSIDE-DOWN CAKE

1¼ cups sifted all-purpose flour	5 maraschino cherries, drained
2 teaspoons baking powder	⅓ cup shortening
¼ teaspoon salt	½ cup granulated sugar
3 tablespoons butter or margarine	1 egg, unbeaten
	1 teaspoon vanilla extract
½ cup packed brown sugar	½ cup syrup drained from pineapple
1 20-ounce can pineapple chunks	

1

About 1½ hours before serving: Preheat oven to 350° F. Sift flour with baking powder, salt. In 8" by 8" by 2" cake pan, melt butter; sprinkle with brown sugar. Drain pineapple chunks, reserving syrup. On brown-sugar mixture, arrange 6 pineapple chunks to form small daisy. Repeat, making 5 daisies in all. (Place remaining chunks between daisies and at edges of pan.) Place cherry in center of each daisy.

2

In large bowl, with electric mixer at medium speed, mix shortening with sugar, then with egg and vanilla, until very light and fluffy—about 4 minutes.

3

At low speed, beat in alternately, just until smooth, flour mixture in thirds and pineapple syrup in halves. Spread batter carefully over pineapple daisies, keeping design intact. Bake cake 1 hour, or until cake tester inserted in center comes out clean. Cool on rack 10 minutes. Then, with spatula, loosen cake from sides of pan. Unmold cake onto serving plate.

4

Serve warm. If desired, top with whipped cream. Makes 6 to 8 servings.

CHECKERBOARD CAKE

T his splendid creation may *look* complicated, but it really isn't. Separate cakes are made from mixes, then put together, checkerboard style, with frosting

---

CHECKERBOARD CAKE

---

1 18½-ounce package
   yellow-cake mix
1 18½- to 19-ounce package
   chocolate-cake mix
½ square unsweetened chocolate

28 to 32 blanched almonds
Butter Cream, opposite
Hungarian Chocolate Frosting,
   opposite

1

Day before, or early in day: Preheat oven to 350° F. Grease, then line with waxed paper, bottom of 16″ by 4″ by 4″ angel-food loaf pan.

2

Make up yellow-cake mix as package label directs. Pour into prepared pan. Bake 40 minutes, or until done. Let cool in pan, on rack, about 1 hour. Remove from pan to rack to finish cooling.

3

Repeat with chocolate-cake mix. Wrap cooled cakes in foil; store.

4

About 1 hour before serving: Melt unsweetened chocolate; into it, dip large end of each almond. Let harden on waxed paper.

5

Make Butter Cream. Slice rounded top from each cake. Halve cakes lengthwise.

6

On foil-covered cardboard, lay four 2-inch-wide strips of waxed paper in rectangle. On it, lay one chocolate-cake strip and one yellow-cake strip, slightly apart, with crusts on outside. Frost cut sides between strips with one fourth of the Butter Cream; press together closely; frost top with two thirds of remaining Butter Cream.

7

Set other two strips on top—chocolate on yellow, yellow on chocolate— use the rest of the Butter Cream to spread between them.

8

Make Hungarian Chocolate Frosting. Lightly frost top and sides of cake to set crumbs. Refrost cake with rest of frosting. On sides of cake, with small spatula, make stroke marks from base to top edge, leaving a small peak at top each time. Then, with same spatula, make zigzag pattern on top of cake as pictured. Remove waxed paper strips. Lay chocolate-tipped almonds along edge of cake as pictured. Makes about 20 servings.

BUTTER CREAM: With mixer at medium speed, or with spoon, thoroughly mix ½ cup soft butter or margarine with ¼ teaspoon salt and 1 cup sifted confectioners' sugar until light and fluffy. Add 3½ cups sifted confectioners' sugar alternately with about ¼ cup milk or light cream, beating until mixture is very smooth and of spreading consistency. Add 2¼ teaspoons vanilla extract.

HUNGARIAN CHOCOLATE FROSTING

---

6 *squares unsweetened chocolate,*	2 *eggs*
melted	½ *cup butter or margarine,*
3 *cups sifted confectioners' sugar*	*softened*

1

In bowl, combine chocolate with sugar and ¼ cup hot water. Add eggs, one at a time, beating well with mixer or spoon. Add butter, 1 tablespoon at a time, beating until thick and of spreading consistency.

JIM'S APPLESAUCE CAKE

    2 cups sifted all-purpose flour
1½ teaspoons baking soda
 ¾ teaspoon salt
 ¾ cup chopped, pitted dates
 ¾ cup dark raisins
 ¾ cup chopped walnuts or
       pecans
 ½ cup shortening

    2 tablespoons cocoa
 ½ teaspoon each: cinnamon,
       ground cloves, nutmeg and
       allspice
1½ cups granulated sugar
    2 eggs, unbeaten
1½ cups canned applesauce

1

Day or so before: Grease 3-quart ring mold on bottom and sides. Sift flour, soda, salt. Toss 2 tablespoons flour mixture with dates, raisins, nuts. Preheat oven to 350° F.

2

In large bowl, with electric mixer at medium speed, mix shortening, cocoa, cinnamon, cloves, nutmeg, allspice. Gradually add sugar, beating until fluffy. Add eggs, one at a time, beating well after each addition. At low speed, beat in alternately, just until smooth, flour mixture and applesauce. Stir in date mixture. Turn into ring mold. Bake 55 to 60 minutes or until cake tester inserted in center comes out clean. Cool in pan 10 minutes; remove from pan; cool on rack. Makes 12 servings.

The best of them all in the nut-cake class. For Christmas, add a crown of candied cherries

NUTCAKE

    3 cups sifted cake flour
1¾ cups granulated sugar
    2 teaspoons double-acting
       baking powder
1½ teaspoons salt
    1 cup shortening
 ¾ cup milk

    2 teaspoons vanilla extract
    4 eggs, unbeaten
    1 cup very finely chopped walnuts
    2 tablespoons light corn syrup
    2 tablespoons butter or margarine
walnut halves for garnish

1

Early in day: Preheat oven to 375° F. Grease, then flour 9-inch tube pan.

Into large bowl, sift flour, sugar, baking powder and salt. Drop in shortening; pour in milk, vanilla and 2 unbeaten eggs. With electric mixer at medium speed, beat 2 minutes. Add remaining eggs, beating 2 minutes. Fold in nuts. Turn batter into tube pan. Bake 60 minutes, or until cake tester inserted in center comes out clean. Set pan on rack; cool 10 to 15 minutes; remove cake. Cool.

3

If desired, glaze as follows: In small saucepan, combine 2 tablespoons corn syrup and 2 tablespoons butter. Boil 3 minutes, *no longer;* drizzle over cake; garnish with few walnut halves. Makes 12 servings.

A cake made from *carrots?* Yes, carrots. They may not make your hair curl, but what they do for the texture and taste of spicecake is simply marvelous

---

SPICY CARROT CAKE

2½ cups sifted all-purpose flour	2½ cups granulated sugar
1½ teaspoons double-acting baking powder	4 eggs, separated
½ teaspoon baking soda	1¾ cups grated raw carrots
¼ teaspoon salt	1 cup chopped pecans
1 teaspoon each: nutmeg, cinnamon, ground cloves	¾ cup sifted confectioners' sugar
1½ cups salad oil	1 tablespoon lemon juice

1

Early in day: Grease well, then flour 10-inch heavy, cast-aluminum bundt pan. Preheat oven to 350° F. Sift together flour, baking powder, baking soda, salt, nutmeg, cinnamon and cloves.

2

In large bowl, with electric mixer at medium speed, cream oil and sugar until well mixed. Beat in egg yolks, one at a time, beating well after each addition. Beat in 5 tablespoons hot water, flour mixture. Into batter, stir 1½ cups of the grated carrots, then pecans. Beat egg whites until soft peaks form; fold into batter. Turn into prepared pan and bake 60 minutes or until a cake tester inserted in center comes out clean. Cool in pan 15 minutes; remove from pan; cool on rack.

3

Combine confectioners' sugar with lemon juice. Drizzle in circle on top of cake. Sprinkle with remaining carrots. Refrigerate. Makes 10 servings.

A dark beauty of a cake, filled with more chocolate, frosted and garnished with chocolate too

LISA'S VELVET LAYER CAKE

½ cup semisweet-chocolate pieces
2 teaspoons shortening
3 cups sifted all-purpose flour
½ cup cocoa
2 teaspoons baking soda
1 teaspoon salt
1 cup butter or margarine
2 cups granulated sugar
2 eggs
vanilla extract

2 cups buttermilk
1 12½-ounce package butter-cream milk-chocolate-frosting mix or 14-ounce package chocolate-fudge-frosting mix
1½ cups heavy or whipping cream
1 tablespoon light corn syrup

1

Day before: In double boiler, over hot, *not boiling,* water, melt chocolate pieces with shortening. Spread on waxed-paper-covered cookie sheet in 8″ by 5″ rectangle; chill until firm. Heat blade of sharp knife in hot water; wipe dry; cut chocolate into two 8″ by 2½″ strips. Cut each crosswise into 4 rectangles, then cut each diagonally into 2 triangles. Chill.

2

Early in day: Grease three 9-inch layer-cake pans; line with waxed paper; grease paper. Sift flour with cocoa, baking soda and salt. Preheat oven to 350° F. In large bowl, with electric mixer at medium speed, beat butter smooth; gradually beat in sugar until fluffy; beat in eggs, one at a time, then 1 teaspoon vanilla.

3

At low speed, beat flour mixture into butter mixture, alternately with buttermilk. Divide among pans. Bake 35 minutes or until cake tester comes out clean. Cool on rack 10 minutes; remove from pans; cool.

4

Into small bowl, measure 1¾ cups of frosting mix; add cream and 1 teaspoon vanilla; refrigerate 45 minutes. With mixer at medium speed, beat chilled mixture until stiff peak form. Use to fill layers.

5

In small bowl, beat rest of package of frosting mix with 2 to 3 tablespoons hot water and corn syrup until it is smooth and spreads. Spread over top of cake; let drizzle down sides as pictured. Garnish top of cake with chocolate triangles; refrigerate. Makes 12 servings.

LISA'S VELVET LAYER CAKE

Another treat for the legions of chocolate lovers—a chocolate buttermilk cake, filled and frosted with a dreamy mixture of honey, chocolate, and cream

CHOCOLATE WHIPPED-CREAM LAYER CAKE

1 *6-ounce package semisweet-*
   chocolate pieces (1 cup)
2¼ *cups sifted all-purpose flour*
1 *teaspoon baking soda*
¾ *teaspoon salt*
¾ *cup butter or margarine*

1¾ *cups granulated sugar*
1 *teaspoon vanilla extract*
3 *eggs*
1 *cup buttermilk*
Dreamy Chocolate Frosting
   (below)

1

Early in day: In double boiler, over hot, *not boiling*, water, stir choco-late pieces with ¼ cup water until melted and blended; remove from heat. Preheat oven to 375° F. Grease, then flour three 8-inch layer-cake pans. Sift flour with baking soda and salt.

2

In large bowl, with electric mixer at medium speed, beat butter with sugar and vanilla until light and fluffy. Beat in eggs, one at a time, until well blended; beat in the melted chocolate.

3

With electric mixer at low speed, beat in alternately flour mixture and buttermilk, beating after each addition until smooth. Divide batter among the three prepared layer-cake pans. Bake 25 minutes or until cake tester inserted in the center of one of the layers comes out clean. Cool cake in pans on racks 10 minutes; carefully loosen edges with spatula; turn cakes out onto racks; cool. Fill and frost with Dreamy Chocolate Frosting. Makes 12 servings.

DREAMY CHOCOLATE FROSTING

1 *6-ounce package semisweet-*
   chocolate pieces (1 cup)

¼ *cup honey*
2 *cups heavy or whipping cream*

1

In double boiler, over hot, *not boiling*, water, melt chocolate with honey and 2 tablespoons water, stirring until smooth. Remove from heat; let stand at room temperature until chocolate feels very cool.

In large bowl, beat cream until it mounds; gradually fold in the cooled chocolate mixture until smooth. Use to fill and frost cooled chocolate layers.

CHOCOLATE-SUNDAE CAKE

4½ cups sifted all-purpose flour	¾ cup butter or margarine
4½ teaspoons double-acting baking powder	¾ cup shortening
	2¼ cups granulated sugar
1½ teaspoons salt	6 eggs, unbeaten
1½ sweet cooking-chocolate bars (¼ pound each)	1½ cups milk
	1½ teaspoons vanilla extract
3 tablespoons light cream	Chocolate Glaze (below)

1

Preheat oven to 350° F. Grease, then flour bottom only of 10-inch tube pan. Sift together flour, baking powder and salt.

2

In double boiler over hot, *not boiling*, water, melt chocolate with 3 tablespoons water until very smooth, stirring occasionally. Remove from heat; blend in light cream.

3

In large bowl, with mixer at medium speed, cream butter with shortening; gradually add sugar; beat until light and fluffy—at least 5 minutes. Beat in eggs, one at a time, beating 1 minute after each addition.

4

Combine milk and vanilla. With mixer at low speed, add dry ingredients alternately with milk, starting and finishing with dry ingredients; beat thoroughly after each addition. Batter will be thick.

5

Turn one-fourth of batter into prepared tube pan; drizzle with a layer of one-third of chocolate mixture. Repeat, alternating layers of batter and chocolate mixture two more times; top with rest of batter. Bake 70 minutes or until cake tester inserted in center comes out clean. Cool in pan 15 minutes; remove from pan to rack; cool. (A crack on top is normal; don't worry.) Spoon Chocolate Glaze (below) along top edge of cake, letting it run down sides.

CHOCOLATE GLAZE

In double boiler over hot, *not boiling*, water, melt 1½ bars sweet cooking chocolate, ¼ pound each, with 2 teaspoons shortening, stirring until smooth.

LANE CAKE

3¼ cups sifted all-purpose flour
3½ teaspoons baking powder
½ teaspoon salt
1 cup butter or margarine
2 cups granulated sugar

1 teaspoon vanilla extract
1 cup milk
8 egg whites
Lane Filling (below)
Lane Frosting (below)

1

Early in day: Preheat oven to 375° F. Grease, then line with waxed paper, bottoms of four 1½-inch deep 9-inch layer-cake pans. Sift flour with baking powder and salt.

2

In large bowl, with electric mixer at medium speed, mix butter with sugar until very light and fluffy. Add vanilla. At low speed, beat in alternately, just until smooth, flour mixture in fourths and milk in thirds.

3

In large bowl, beat egg whites until they form stiff peaks. Gently fold batter into egg whites. Turn into pans. Bake 20 minutes, or until cake tester inserted in center comes out clean. Cool. Fill; frost.

LANE FILLING

8 egg yolks
1¼ cups granulated sugar
½ cup butter or margarine
1 cup chopped pecans

1 cup canned flaked coconut
1 cup cut-up candied cherries
⅓ cup whiskey or wine
1 cup finely chopped raisins

1

In saucepan, beat egg yolks slightly. Cook with sugar and butter over low heat, stirring, about 5 minutes or until slightly thickened. Add remaining ingredients. Cool; spread between cake layers.

LANE FROSTING

2½ cups granulated sugar
⅛ teaspoon salt
⅓ cup dark corn syrup

2 egg whites
1 teaspoon vanilla extract

1

In saucepan, combine sugar, salt, corn syrup, ⅔ cup water. Cook over low heat, stirring, until sugar is dissolved. Bring to boiling, uncovered. Don't stir.

In small bowl, with electric mixer at high speed, beat egg whites until foamy; add 3 tablespoons syrup mixture, beating until stiff but not dry. Boil rest of syrup to 240° F. on candy thermometer or until it spins a thread from spoon. Pour slowly over egg whites, beating until frosting begins to lose gloss and hold shape. Add vanilla. Spread frosting over top and sides of filled cake layers, adding a drop or two of hot water if it becomes too thick.

Moist, delicate, and tasting faintly of orange, our marble cake deserves its deluxe rating

DELUXE MARBLE CAKE

2 squares unsweetened chocolate	½ teaspoon salt
granulated sugar	½ teaspoon baking soda
1 teaspoon vanilla extract	½ cup butter or margarine
2 cups sifted all-purpose flour	3 eggs
2 teaspoons double-acting	¾ cup undiluted evaporated milk
baking powder	1 teaspoon orange extract

1

Early in day: Preheat oven to 350° F. In small saucepan over very low heat, melt chocolate with ¼ cup granulated sugar and ¼ cup water while stirring; stir in vanilla extract; cool. Sift flour with baking powder, salt and baking soda.

2

In large bowl, with electric mixer at medium speed, cream butter with 1 cup granulated sugar until fluffy; beat in eggs, one at a time. At low speed, gradually beat in flour mixture alternately wtih evaporated milk; add orange extract. Combine about 1½ cups of the cake batter with prepared chocolate mixture.

3

Into well-greased and floured 9-inch springform cake pan, alternately spoon chocolate and yellow batters; with knife, cut through batter a few times. Bake 55 minutes, or until cake tester inserted in center comes out clean. Cool in pan 10 minutes; remove from pan; cool on rack. Makes 12 servings.

SUGAR BUSH WALNUT CAKE

M

ocha cream, quickly made with instant coffee, tops a chiffon-light walnut confection

SUGAR BUSH WALNUT CAKE

2¼ cups sifted all-purpose
     flour
granulated sugar
  3 teaspoons double-acting
     baking powder
  1 teaspoon salt
  ½ cup salad oil
  7 eggs, separated

  1 teaspoon vanilla extract
  1 teaspoon maple extract
  ⅔ cup finely chopped walnuts
  ½ teaspoon cream of tartar
  1 cup heavy or whipping cream
  1 tablespoon instant coffee
 12 walnut halves for garnish

1

Early in day: Preheat oven to 325° F. In large bowl, place flour, 1½ cups sugar, baking powder, salt, salad oil, ¾ cup cold water, egg yolks and extracts. With mixer at medium speed, beat until smooth; stir in chopped walnuts. Pour batter into 3-quart mixing bowl.

2

In large bowl, beat egg whites for 1 minute at high speed. Add cream of tartar; continue beating until whites are very stiff. Gently fold stiffly beaten egg whites into batter. Pour batter into ungreased 4-inch-deep, 10-inch tube pan. Bake cake 55 minutes, then raise oven heat to 350° F. and bake 20 minutes longer. Gently press top of cake with finger; if it does not spring back, bake 5 minutes longer.

3

Invert pan and let cake hang in pan for 1 hour or until cold. Never remove cake from pan while warm; it will shrink. Insert spatula between cake and side of pan to loosen. Invert cake on cake plate.

4

About 15 minutes before serving: In bowl, combine heavy cream, instant coffee, 1 tablespoon sugar. With rotary beater, beat until stiff enough to spread. Swirl over top of cake. Arrange walnut halves on top. Makes 12 servings.

---

nother featherweight cake, this one with the delightful fragrance and flavor of oranges

---

BIG ORANGE CHIFFON

2¼ cups sifted cake flour	3 tablespoons grated orange peel
1½ cups granulated sugar	¾ cup orange juice
3 teaspoons double-acting baking powder	7 or 8 egg whites, room temperature
1 teaspoon salt	¾ cup orange juice
½ cup salad oil	½ teaspoon cream of tartar
5 medium egg yolks, unbeaten	

1

About 2 hours before serving: Into large bowl, sift flour, sugar, baking powder, salt. Make well in flour mixture; pour salad oil in well. Add egg yolks, orange peel, orange juice. With electric mixer at medium speed, beat until smooth. Preheat oven to 325°F.

2

Into large bowl, with electric mixer at high speed, beat egg whites with cream of tartar until very stiff peaks form. Do not underbeat. Slowly pour egg-yolk mixture over whites, folding in mixture gently with rubber spatula or spoon until mixture is just blended. Turn into ungreased 4-inch-deep, 10″ tube pan. Bake at 325° F. 55 minutes, then at 350° F. 10 to 15 minutes, or until cake tester inserted in center comes out clean. Invert cake and let it hang in pan for 1 hour. Insert spatula between cake and side of pan. Invert on plate. Makes 12 servings.

---

offee flavors both the cake and its nut-strewn icing, making it a favorite with lovers of the brew. Naturally it tastes great with a cup of the same

COFFEE CLOUD CAKE

1 tablespoon instant coffee
1 cup boiling water
2 cups sifted all-purpose flour
3 teaspoons double-acting
  baking powder
½ teaspoon salt
6 egg whites
½ teaspoon cream of tartar

granulated sugar
  6 egg yolks
  1 teaspoon vanilla extract
  1 cup finely chopped walnuts
Coffee Icing (below)
1½ cups coarsely chopped
  walnuts

1

Early in day: Stir coffee into boiling water to dissolve; cool. Preheat oven to 350° F. Sift flour with baking powder and salt.

2

In large bowl, beat egg whites with cream of tartar until soft peaks begin to form; add ½ cup granulated sugar, 2 tablespoons at a time, continuing to beat until very stiff and straight peaks are formed. Do not underbeat. Set aside.

3

In large bowl, beat egg yolks until blended; gradually beat in 1½ cups granulated sugar and vanilla. Now beat at high speed until thick and lemon-colored, 5 to 10 minutes.

4

To egg-yolk mixture, add flour mixture alternately with cooled coffee, beginning and ending with flour mixture. Fold in finely chopped walnuts. Fold egg-yolk mixture into stiffly beaten egg whites, one fourth at a time, using no more than 15 strokes for each addition. After last addition, continue folding just until evenly blended. Pour batter into ungreased 10″ tube pan. Bake 60 to 70 minutes or until cake springs back when touched lightly with finger.

5

Invert cake and let it hang in pan for 1 hour or until cold. Insert spatula all the way around sides of pan to loosen cake. Invert cake on cake plate. Lift off pan. Frost with Coffee Icing and garnish with nuts. Makes 12 servings.

COFFEE ICING: In medium bowl, combine one 16-ounce box confectioners' sugar, 2 tablespoons instant coffee, 1 egg or 2 egg yolks, 1 tablespoon butter or margarine, softened and 2 to 3 tablespoons milk. With electric mixer at medium speed, beat 5 minutes or until smooth and easy to spread. Makes 1¾ cups frosting.

Freshly baked spongecake, filled with a delectable combination of strawberries and cream, keeps pulling in votes as the most delicious dessert ever

---

STRAWBERRY ROLL

¾ cup sifted cake flour
¾ teaspoon double-acting
   baking powder
¼ teaspoon salt
 4 eggs, at room temperature
¾ cup granulated sugar

1 teaspoon vanilla extract
confectioners' sugar
1 cup heavy or whipping cream,
   whipped
2 cups sliced fresh strawberries

1

Early in day: Preheat oven to 400° F. Line bottom of 15½″ by 10½″ by 1″ jelly-roll pan with waxed paper. Sift flour with baking powder and salt.

2

In bowl, with mixer at high speed, beat eggs until foamy. Beat in granulated sugar gradually; continue beating until very thick and light-colored. With rubber spatula or spoon, fold in flour mixture and vanilla. Spread in prepared pan. Bake 13 minutes or until light brown. Lightly dust clean dish towel with confectioners' sugar. When cake is done, loosen sides from pan with spatula; invert onto towel. Lift off pan; carefully peel off paper. With knife, cut any crisp edges from cake. Starting with narrow end, roll cake very gently, rolling towel in it (this prevents cake from sticking) ; cool.

3

About 1 hour and 15 minutes before serving: Unroll cake flat on towel. Spread with whipped cream; sprinkle with berries. Roll up cake from narrow end; place roll, seam side down, on serving plate; refrigerate.

Just before serving: Sprinkle roll generously with confectioners' sugar. Cut into 1-inch crosswise slices. Makes 8 servings.

CHOCOLATE ROLL

½ cup sifted cake flour
½ teaspoon double-acting
   baking powder
¼ teaspoon salt
 2 squares unsweetened chocolate
¾ cup sifted granulated sugar
 4 eggs, at room temperature

1 teaspoon vanilla extract
2 tablespoons granulated sugar
¼ teaspoon baking soda
confectioners' sugar
¼ teaspoon almond extract
1 cup heavy or whipping
   cream, whipped

1

Early in day: Grease 15½" by 10½" by 1" jelly-roll pan; line bottom of pan with waxed paper. Sift flour with baking powder and salt. Preheat oven to 375° F. Melt chocolate in double boiler over hot, *not boiling,* water.

2

In large bowl, sift ¾ cup sugar over eggs; with electric mixer at high speed, beat until very thick and light. Fold flour mixture and vanilla, all at once, into egg mixture.

3

To melted chocolate, add 2 tablespoons sugar, soda, 3 tablespoons cold water; stir until thick and light; quickly fold into batter; turn into pan. Bake 15 minutes or just until cake springs back when gently touched.

4

Place clean dish towel on flat surface; over it, sift thick layer of confectioners' sugar. When cake is done, loosen it from sides of pan, invert onto towel. Lift off pan; carefully peel off paper; with very sharp knife, cut crisp edges from cake, to make rolling easier. Cool 5 minutes. Fold hem of towel over edge of cake. Roll up cake very gently from narrow end, rolling towel up in it (this prevents cake from sticking). Gently lift rolled cake onto rack to cool—about 1 hour. (If cake is warm, whipped-cream filling will melt.)

5

Just before serving: Carefully unroll cake on towel. Add almond extract to whipped cream; quickly spread over cake to within 1" of edges. Start rolling up cake from narrow end by folding edge of cake over, then tucking it under; continue rolling cake, lifting towel higher and higher with one hand as you guide roll with other hand. Finish with open end of cake on underside. Makes 10 servings.

GERMAN GOLD CAKE RING

3½ cups sifted cake flour
1½ teaspoons double-acting
    baking powder
⅛ teaspoon salt
1 cup butter or margarine

2 cups granulated sugar
6 egg yolks
2 teaspoons vanilla extract
1 cup milk

1

Early in day: Preheat oven to 350° F. Sift together flour, baking powder, salt. Grease, then flour, 3-quart fluted ring mold.

2

In large bowl, with electric mixer at high speed, mix butter with sugar, then with egg yolks and vanilla, adding them gradually until very light, fluffy. At low speed, beat in alternately, until smooth, flour mixture in fourths, milk in thirds. Turn batter into ring mold. Bake 1 hour or until cake tester inserted in center comes out clean; cool in pan 10 minutes; remove from pan; cool on rack. If desired, fill center with scoops of ice cream, drizzle with caramel sauce. Makes 12 servings.

DUNDEE CAKE

1 cup butter or margarine
⅔ cup granulated sugar
4 eggs
2½ cups sifted cake flour
1 teaspoon double-acting
    baking powder
½ teaspoon salt
1 cup currants
½ cup dark raisins

½ cup finely chopped candied
    citron
1¼ cups blanched almonds,
    coarsely chopped
grated peel 1 lemon
2 tablespoons grated orange
    peel
2 tablespoons orange juice

1

Up to 3 days ahead: In large bowl, with electric mixer at medium speed, beat butter and sugar until creamy; then beat in eggs, one at a time, until fluffy. Preheat oven to 325° F.

2

Sift together flour, baking powder and salt; stir in currants and next 5 ingredients. Beat into butter mixture alternately with juice. Pour into greased 10″ by 5″ by 3″ loaf pan. Bake 70 minutes or until cake tester inserted in center comes out clean. Cool in pan 10 minutes; turn out on rack; cool. Wrap in foil. Makes 1 loaf.

RUM CAKE DE MAISON

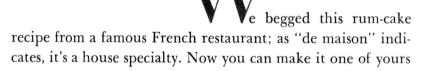

W e begged this rum-cake
recipe from a famous French restaurant; as "de maison" indi-
cates, it's a house specialty. Now you can make it one of yours

---

RUM CAKE DE MAISON

2 *cups sifted cake flour*
2 *teaspoons double-acting*
  baking powder
¼ *teaspoon salt*
¼ *teaspoon baking soda*
½ *cup butter or margarine*
granulated sugar
2 *eggs, separated*
1 *teaspoon grated orange peel*

½ *cup orange juice*
white rum
¼ *teaspoon almond extract*
¼ *teaspoon vanilla extract*
Whipped Cream Filling
  (opposite)
Chocolate Frosting (opposite)
1½ *cups coarsely chopped*
  walnuts

1

Day before: Grease two 9-inch, 1½-inch-deep layer-cake pans; line bottoms with circle of waxed paper. Preheat oven to 350° F. Sift together
flour, baking powder, salt and baking soda.

In large bowl, with mixer at medium speed, beat butter until very soft and creamy; gradually beat in ¾ cup sugar, then continue beating until light and fluffy. Beat in egg yolks, one at a time, then orange peel. Combine orange juice with 3 tablespoons rum and extracts; add alternately with flour mixture to creamed mixture, while beating at low speed.

In medium bowl, beat egg whites to soft peaks; gradually beat in ¼ cup sugar, then continue beating to stiff peaks. Fold batter into whites, then pour into pans. Bake 25 minutes or until top springs back when pressed gently with finger. Cool in pans on racks about 10 minutes; remove from pans; cool. Meanwhile, make Whipped Cream Filling and Chocolate Frosting.

With long, sharp knife, split cooled layers horizontally to make 4 layers in all. Sprinkle each layer with 2 tablespoons rum. On cake plate, put layers together, using about ¾ cup Whipped Cream Filling between each layer. Refrigerate cake while making Chocolate Frosting. Use to frost sides and top of cake, then press walnuts into frosting all around sides of cake. Refrigerate cake until serving time—at least 18 hours. Makes 16 luscious servings.

WHIPPED CREAM FILLING: While cakes are cooling, place medium bowl and beaters in freezer until cold. In double boiler, sprinkle 2 teaspoons unflavored gelatin over 2 tablespoons cold water; place over hot, *not boiling,* water; heat until gelatin is dissolved; cool slightly. In cold bowl, combine 2 cups heavy or whipping cream with ½ cup confectioners' sugar; combine ⅓ cup white rum and gelatin. Stir into cream; beat until just stiff enough to hold its shape. Use to fill cakes. Makes 4½ cups.

CHOCOLATE FROSTING: In double boiler, over hot, *not boiling,* water, melt 4 squares unsweetened chocolate; remove from heat. With electric mixer, gradually beat in 1 cup confectioners' sugar and 2 tablespoons hot water. Then beat in 2 eggs, one at a time, and then 6 tablespoons soft butter or margarine, 2 tablespoons at a time; continue beating until smooth, light in color and of spreading consistency. Use to frost top and sides of 9-inch layer cake.

Few gifts are more welcome than a fruitcake. This recipe yields six, in assorted sizes

ETHEL'S FRUITCAKE

4 cups sifted all-purpose flour
1 teaspoon baking soda
2 teaspoons cinnamon
1 teaspoon nutmeg
1 teaspoon ground cloves
1 pound dried figs, finely chopped
1 pound pitted dates, finely chopped
1 pound preserved pineapple, diced
¼ pound each: preserved orange peel, preserved lemon peel, and citron, diced
1 pound candied cherries, chopped
½ pound blanched almonds, finely chopped
½ pound pecans, coarsely chopped
1 15-ounce package golden raisins
2 1-pound packages dark raisins
1 pound butter or margarine, softened
2 cups packed brown sugar
12 egg yolks
½ cup canned pineapple juice
½ cup light molasses
12 egg whites

1

Make a month or so ahead, early in day: Sift together flour, baking soda, cinnamon, nutmeg and cloves. In large bowl, thoroughly mix figs, and next 10 ingredients; add 2 cups of the sifted flour mixture. With waxed paper, snugly line well-greased 5½" by 3" by 2¼" loaf pan; two 6" by 3½" round tea or coffee cans; two 7½" by 3½" by 2¼" loaf pans; and one 2-quart casserole. Lightly grease waxed paper.

2

Preheat oven to 275° F. In large bowl, with electric mixer at medium speed, beat butter and brown sugar until fluffy. Mix in egg yolks. Mix in alternately, just until smooth, remaining flour mixture, juice and molasses. Turn mixture into large kettle; stir in fruit mixture by hand.

3

Beat egg whites until they form soft peaks; fold into cake mixture. Turn mixture into prepared pans, filling two thirds full.

4

Bake 3 loaf cakes 2 to 2½ hours; bake 2 round cakes 2½ to 3 hours; bake casserole cake, covered, 2 hours; uncover, then bake 45 minutes more. Cakes are done when cake tester inserted in center comes out clean.

Completely cool cakes in pan; remove, then remove paper. Wrap cakes tightly in plastic wrap or foil; refrigerate. If desired, unwrap occasionally and brush with cider, port, sherry or brandy.

Lighter in texture than traditional dark fruitcakes, the golden kind is preferred by some

---

GOLDEN FRUITCAKE

2 cups golden raisins (or half dark raisins)
1 cup each: candied citron, lemon peel and orange peel
½ cup candied pineapple
½ cup halved candied cherries
1½ cups chopped dried figs
1 cup chopped pitted dates
½ cup currants
1 cup halved blanched almonds, pecans or walnuts

4 cups sifted all-purpose flour
½ teaspoon salt
2 teaspoons double-acting baking powder
1 cup butter or margarine
2 cups granulated sugar
6 eggs, unbeaten
1 teaspoon lemon or orange extract
1 cup sherry or orange juice

1

Make several weeks ahead: Line 10-inch, 4-inch-deep angel-food pan with foil. Preheat oven to 300° F.

2

In large bowl, combine first 10 ingredients. Over them, sift flour with salt, baking powder; toss lightly until fruits and nuts are well coated.

3

In larger bowl, with electric mixer at medium speed, mix butter with sugar, then with eggs and extract, until very light and fluffy—about 4 minutes. Then, with spoon, stir in fruit-and-nut mixture, alternately with sherry, just until mixed.

4

Turn batter into angel-food pan. Bake 3 hours or till cake tester inserted in center of fruitcake comes out clean and dry. Cool cake completely in pan on rack; remove it from pan; wrap well with foil or plastic wrap; refrigerate till needed. Or freezer-wrap and freeze. Makes 1 cake.

MINIATURE FRUITCAKES

4 cups sifted all-purpose flour
3 teaspoons double-acting
  baking powder
1 teaspoon salt
½ teaspoon ground nutmeg
½ pound each: diced and
  preserved citron, orange peel
  and pineapple
½ pound whole candied cherries
1 15-ounce package golden

raisins
1½ cups canned slivered toasted
  almonds
1 7-ounce package fine grated
  coconut
1½ cups butter or margarine
1½ cups granulated sugar
1 cup canned pineapple juice
10 egg whites

1

Several days ahead: Line cupcake-pan cups with foil nut cups or cup-cake liners. Sift flour with baking powder, salt, nutmeg. In large bowl or pan, mix citron and next 6 ingredients; add flour mixture; stir to coat fruits well. In 4½-quart bowl, cream butter with spoon or mixer till creamy; gradually beat in sugar till light, fluffy. Stir in floured fruit mixture alternately with pineapple juice, starting and ending with fruit.

2

Preheat oven to 325° F. In large bowl with electric mixer at high speed, beat egg whites stiff; carefully fold them into batter until no egg-white flecks remain. Put rounded measuring tablespoon of batter in each lined cupcake cup. Bake 40 minutes or until done; cool on rack; repeat until all batter is used. Cool. Makes 100.

DOUBLE-CHOCOLATE MINIATURE CAKES

1 3-ounce package cream
  cheese, softened
1 egg
1 egg yolk
granulated sugar
salt
½ cup semisweet-chocolate
  pieces
1½ cups sifted all-purpose flour

¼ cup cocoa
¾ teaspoon baking soda
⅓ cup salad oil
1 egg white
1 tablespoon vinegar
1 teaspoon vanilla extract
¾ cup toasted, slivered almonds,
  chopped

1

Early in day: Preheat oven to 350° F. Line twelve 3-inch cupcake-pan cups with paper liners. In small bowl, with electric mixer at medium speed, beat cream cheese, egg, egg yolk, ¼ cup granulated sugar and dash of salt until smooth; stir in chocolate pieces. Set aside.

Into large bowl, sift together flour, 1 cup granulated sugar, cocoa, baking soda, ½ teaspoon salt.

Combine ¾ cup water, salad oil, egg white, vinegar and vanilla; beat well with fork. Add, all at once, to dry ingredients; stir with spoon until well mixed. Fill each prepared cupcake-pan cup about half full with cocoa batter. Onto center of each, spoon 1 tablespoon of cream-cheese mixture. Generously sprinkle tops with about 1 tablespoon granulated sugar, then with almonds. Bake 25 minutes or until cupcakes are golden. Cool in pans 10 minutes; remove to rack; cool. Makes 12.

KENTUCKY CUPCAKES

1½ cups sifted all-purpose flour	2 tablespoons fruit juice
1 teaspoon allspice	½ cup seedless black raspberry
¼ teaspoon cinnamon	preserves
1½ teaspoons baking soda	2 squares unsweetened
⅓ cup shortening	chocolate, melted
½ cup granulated sugar	½ cup golden or dark raisins
½ cup packed brown sugar	½ cup currants
2 eggs, separated	½ cup chopped walnuts
¾ cup buttermilk	

1

Early in day: Preheat oven to 350° F. Line sixteen 3-inch cupcake-pan cups with paper liners. Sift together flour, allspice, cinnamon and baking soda.

2

In large bowl, with electric mixer at medium speed, mix shortening with sugars, then with egg yolks, until light and fluffy—about 4 minutes. Combine buttermilk and juice. At low speed, add to egg-yolk mixture, alternately with flour mixture. Begin and end with flour mixture; beat just until blended. Add preserves and melted chocolate; blend thoroughly. Fold in raisins, currants, and walnuts.

3

In small bowl, with electric mixer at high speed, beat egg whites until stiff but not dry. Fold into batter; pour into prepared cupcake-pan cups. Bake 25 minutes or until done. Remove from pans; cool on racks. If desired, frost with fluffy white frosting. Makes 16.

T he same Max responsible for the Spinach-and-Bacon Salad on page 28 also dreamed up this speedy but delicious cheese pie with its sour cream topping

MAX'S SUPER CHEESE PIE

1⅓ cups packaged graham-
  cracker crumbs
⅓ cup packed brown sugar
½ teaspoon cinnamon
⅓ cup melted butter or
  margarine
1½ 8-ounce packages cream

  cheese, softened
2 eggs
½ cup granulated sugar
½ teaspoon vanilla extract
1 cup sour cream
12 fresh strawberries

1

About 4 hours before serving: In well-greased 9-inch pie plate, mix graham-cracker crumbs, brown sugar, cinnamon and butter until crumbly. With back of spoon, press to bottom and sides of pie plate. Refrigerate.

2

Preheat oven to 350° F. In small bowl, beat together cream cheese, eggs, sugar and vanilla until smooth and creamy. Turn this mixture into crumb crust. Bake 35 minutes or until firm; remove to rack.

3

Spread sour cream on top and allow pie to cool. Serve as is, or topped with strawberries, quartered lengthwise. Makes 8 to 10 servings.

To make ahead: Make the cheese pie ahead of time, leaving off the sour cream and strawberries. Then freezer-wrap and freeze. About four hours before serving, thaw the pie at room temperature, spread with sour cream and garnish with strawberries.

CHERRY GLAZE: Mix 2½ teaspoons cornstarch with 2 tablespoons sugar; slowly stir in ½ cup liquid drained from canned pitted sour red cherries, packed in water; simmer until clear and thickened. Add 1 cup drained pitted cherries, 1 teaspoon lemon juice, ¼ teaspoon almond extract, few drops red food color. Cool.

PINEAPPLE GLAZE: Combine 1 cup canned crushed pineapple and 1 teaspoon cornstarch. Simmer until clear and thickened; add 1 tablespoon lemon juice. Cool.

W

hat would you call golden meringue, filled with lemon custard and whipped cream? *We* call it heavenly, especially when garnished with strawberries

---

HEAVENLY PIE

---

granulated sugar
¼ teaspoon cream of tartar
4 eggs, separated
canned flaked coconut

⅛ teaspoon salt
1 tablespoon grated lemon peel
3 tablespoons lemon juice
2 cups heavy or whipping cream

1

Day before: Sift together 1 cup sugar and cream of tartar. Preheat oven to 275° F.

2

In large bowl, with electric mixer at high speed, beat egg whites until they form stiff, but not dry peaks. Slowly add sugar mixture, beating until very stiff, glossy peaks form; spread this meringue over bottom and up sides, just to rim, of well-greased 9-inch pie plate, making bottom ¼-inch thick, sides 1-inch thick. Sprinkle top edge with 2 tablespoons coconut. Bake 1 hour or until golden and crisp; cool.

3

Meanwhile, in double boiler, beat egg yolks slightly; stir in ½ cup sugar, salt, lemon peel and juice; set over boiling water; cook, stirring constantly, until thick custard forms—about 10 minutes. Cool.

4

Whip 1 cup of the heavy cream; fold cooled custard into it. Pour lemon-cream mixture into cooled meringue crust. Smooth top with spatula. Refrigerate at least 12 hours, preferably 24 hours.

5

At serving time: Top pie with 1 cup heavy cream, whipped. Makes 8 servings.

CHOCOLATE CREAM PIE

---

1 baked 9-inch pie shell
3¼ cups milk
granulated sugar
¼ cup butter or margarine
6 tablespoons cocoa
5 tablespoons cornstarch

½ teaspoon salt
1 teaspoon vanilla extract
4 egg yolks, beaten
¾ cup heavy or whipping cream
shaved unsweetened chocolate

1

Early in day: In saucepan, scald milk with ½ cup sugar and butter. Meanwhile, in small bowl, combine ¼ cup sugar, cocoa, cornstarch and salt. To cocoa mixture, add some of hot milk, then vanilla, while stirring constantly. Return all to saucepan; cook over low heat, stirring, until mixture is smooth and thickened and comes to a boil. Preheat oven to 300° F.

2

Into beaten egg yolks, stir some of hot cocoa mixture; return all to saucepan. Cook, stirring, about 2 minutes. Into pie shell, turn chocolate filling. Bake 1 hour; cool; refrigerate.

3

At serving time: Whip cream; fold in 1 teaspoon sugar; spread on pie. Sprinkle cream with shaved chocolate. Makes 8 servings.

FRESH APPLE PIE

pastry for 9-inch two-crust pie
⅔ to ¾ cup granulated sugar (or half granulated and half brown sugar)
1 to 2 tablespoons flour (if fruit is very juicy)
½ teaspoon grated lemon peel
1 to 2 teaspoons lemon juice
½ teaspoon cinnamon
¼ teaspoon nutmeg
⅛ teaspoon salt
6 to 7 cups thinly sliced, pared, cored cooking apples (2 pounds)
1 tablespoon butter or margarine

1

Roll out half of pastry to line 9-inch pie plate; refrigerate. Preheat oven to 425° F.

2

Combine sugar with flour, lemon peel and juice, cinnamon, nutmeg and salt (amount depends on tartness of apples).

3

Place half of apples in pastry-lined pie plate, with sharp edges facing inward; sprinkle with half of sugar mixture. Top with rest of apples, heaping them in center, then with rest of sugar mixture. Dot with butter.

4

Trim bottom pastry even with rim of pie plate, using scissors or knife. Moisten edge of pastry with water. Roll out rest of pastry, then fit, seal; make slits in top. Bake 40 to 50 minutes, or until crust is nicely browned; cool. Makes 8 servings.

SOUTHERN PEANUT-BUTTER PIE

SOUTHERN PEANUT-BUTTER PIE

Creamy, crunchy, salty-sweet,
this pie is a favorite with children North, South, East, West

---

SOUTHERN PEANUT-BUTTER PIE

1 unbaked 9-inch pie shell
3 eggs
1 cup dark corn syrup
½ cup granulated sugar

½ cup creamy-style peanut butter
½ teaspoon vanilla extract
1 cup salted peanuts

1

Early in day: Preheat oven to 400° F. In large bowl, with electric mixer at medium speed, beat eggs with corn syrup, sugar, peanut butter and vanilla till smooth, then stir in peanuts.

2

Pour filling into pie shell; bake 15 minutes. Lower oven heat to 350° F.; bake pie 30 to 35 minutes or until it is set and top is golden brown. Cool on rack. Makes 8 servings.

FIRST-LADY PECAN PIE

1 unbaked 9-inch pie shell
1 cup granulated sugar
½ teaspoon salt
1 cup dark corn syrup
3 eggs

½ cup butter or margarine
1½ teaspoons vanilla extract
2 cups coarsely chopped pecans
1 cup heavy or whipping cream,
  whipped (optional)

1

Make day or two before: Preheat oven to 325° F. In saucepan, combine granulated sugar, salt, corn syrup; simmer until sugar dissolves. Meanwhile, beat eggs foamy.

2

Into syrup, stir butter, vanilla and chopped pecans. When butter melts, stir in eggs; turn into pie shell.

3

Bake 40 minutes; remove to rack; cool; refrigerate. Serve with or without cream. Makes 8 servings.

HONEY-WALNUT PUMPKIN PIE

1 unbaked 9-inch pie shell
4 eggs, separated
1 cup packed light brown sugar
½ teaspoon each: cinnamon,
  nutmeg, allspice
2 cups canned pumpkin

⅓ cup heavy or whipping cream
¼ cup butter or margarine,
  melted
1 tablespoon cornstarch
⅓ cup honey
⅓ cup chopped walnuts

1

Early in day: In large bowl, with electric mixer at high speed, beat yolks and sugar until thick and lemon-colored. At low speed, beat in spices, then pumpkin, cream and butter. Preheat oven to 450° F.

2

In medium bowl, beat egg whites until frothy; gradually add cornstarch, beating until stiff but not dry; fold into pumpkin mixture; pour into pie shell. Bake 15 minutes; reduce oven heat to 350° F.; bake 30 minutes or until knife inserted in center comes out clean. Cool; refrigerate.

3

At serving time: Mix honey and nuts; spread on pie. Makes 8 servings.

FROSTED DAIQUIRI PIE

1 baked 9-inch pie shell
1 envelope unflavored gelatin
granulated sugar
½ teaspoon salt
3 eggs, separated
½ cup lime juice

1 teaspoon grated lime or lemon
  peel
green food color
⅓ cup light rum
whipped cream for garnish

1

Early in day: In double boiler, combine gelatin with ⅔ cup sugar and salt; add egg yolks, ¼ cup cold water, lime juice; with rotary beater, beat until blended. Cook over boiling water (or in saucepan over low heat), stirring, until mixture coats spoon. Remove from heat; add peel; tint pale green. Cool mixture; stir in rum. Refrigerate until slightly thicker than unbeaten egg white.

2

In large bowl, with electric mixer at high speed, beat egg whites until they form moist peaks when beater is raised; then add ⅓ cup sugar, 1 tablespoon at a time, beating until stiff. Fold in gelatin mixture; turn into pie shell; refrigerate. Top with whipped cream, sweetened if desired. Makes 8 servings.

A delicate coffee gelatin, flavored with crème de menthe, is mixed with egg white and whipped cream, then poured into a chocolate-crumb crust

GRASSHOPPER PIE

1½ cups chocolate wafer crumbs
3 tablespoons butter, melted
1 envelope unflavored gelatin
granulated sugar
⅛ teaspoon salt

3 eggs, separated
¼ cup crème de menthe
¼ cup coffee, cooled
1 cup heavy or whipping
  cream, whipped

1

Day before serving: Preheat oven to 375° F. In small bowl, combine chocolate crumbs and butter; press evenly into bottom and up sides of 9-inch pie plate. Bake 8 minutes; cool.

In medium saucepan, sprinkle gelatin over ½ cup cold water. Add ¼ cup sugar, salt and well-beaten egg yolks, stirring, until well-blended. Cook over low heat, stirring constantly, until gelatin dissolves and mixture thickens, about 10 minutes. Remove from heat; stir in crème de menthe and coffee. Refrigerate, stirring often, until mixture resembles consistency of unbeaten egg whites, about 20 minutes.

3

In small bowl, with electric mixer at high speed, beat egg whites until stiff but not dry; gradually beat in ¼ cup sugar, beating until very stiff peaks form. Fold into gelatin mixture with whipped cream until well blended. Pour into crust; refrigerate. Makes 10 servings.

A real boon for busy cooks, this pie retains its dreamy texture and taste in the freezer

FROZEN CHOCOLATE VELVET PIE

2 egg whites
⅛ teaspoon salt
¼ cup granulated sugar
2 cups finely chopped walnuts
¼ cup light corn syrup
1 tablespoon vanilla extract

1 cup semisweet-chocolate pieces
⅔ cup canned, sweetened condensed milk, chilled
1½ cups heavy or whipping cream

1

Make and freeze up to 1 month ahead: Preheat oven to 400° F. Beat egg whites with salt until soft peaks form when beater is raised. Gradually beat in sugar; beat until stiff peaks form; add nuts; spread over bottom and up sides of greased 8-inch pie plate, making rim ¾ inch high. Bake 12 minutes; cool.

2

Meanwhile, bring corn syrup and 1 tablespoon water just to boiling, stirring. Remove from heat; stir in vanilla, then chocolate until it is melted; cool. Reserve 2 tablespoons of this chocolate mixture; pour rest into large bowl with condensed milk and cream. With electric mixer at low speed, blend mixture well; at medium speed, beat until soft peaks form when beater is raised. Pour filling into cooled pie shell. Place, unwrapped, in freezer until firm. When pie is firm, drizzle on reserved chocolate. Freezer-wrap and freeze up to 1 month. Remove from freezer just before serving dinner; unwrap; refrigerate until dessert time. Makes 6 servings.

T he crust is made of gingersnap crumbs; beneath the cream topping there's a layer of rum custard. The black bottom? Velvety chocolate custard

BLACK-BOTTOM PIE

1⅓ cups fine gingersnap crumbs
⅓ cup melted butter or margarine
1 3¼-ounce package vanilla pudding-and-pie-filling mix
1 envelope unflavored gelatin
2 egg yolks
1½ cups milk

2 squares unsweetened chocolate
3 egg whites
pinch cream of tartar
¼ cup granulated sugar
2 tablespoons rum
½ cup heavy cream, whipped
9 gingersnap halves

1

Early in day: Into electric-blender container, place 6 gingersnaps at a time, broken into pieces; blend at low speed until only a few coarse crumbs remain. Or lay cookies between two sheets of waxed paper; using rolling pin, crush cookies.

2

Preheat oven to 300° F. Mix crumbs with butter. Press into 8-inch pie plate. Bake 10 minutes. Cool.

3

Meanwhile, combine pudding mix with gelatin; beat together yolks and milk. Stir into pudding in saucepan. Stir, over low heat, until thickened.

4

In double boiler; over hot, *not boiling,* water, melt 1½ squares unsweetened chocolate. Stir in half of pudding mixture until smooth; spoon into crust. With waxed paper, cover rest of mixture; chill until just beginning to set.

5

Meanwhile, beat egg whites with cream of tartar until soft, moist peaks are formed when beaters are raised. Now add sugar gradually, beating until stiff. Carefully fold in remaining pudding and rum. Pour as much of egg-white mixture on chocolate layer as shell will hold; refrigerate a few minutes, then pile rest on top. Chill until set.

6

To serve: Top with whipped cream. Insert gingersnaps on top; shave on ½ square chocolate. Makes 8 servings.

BLACK-BOTTOM PIE

For the grand feast of them all, a feather-light pie flavored with glacéed cherries and rum, then garnished with whipped cream and Brazil nuts

CHRISTMAS PIE

1½ cups Brazil-nut meats*
  3 tablespoons granulated sugar
  1 envelope unflavored gelatin
granulated sugar
  ⅛ teaspoon salt
  3 eggs, separated
1¾ cups milk, scalded

¼ to ⅓ cup glacéed cherries, thinly sliced
3 tablespoons white rum or 2 teaspoons vanilla extract
¾ to 1 cup heavy or whipping cream

1

Day before, or early in day: Preheat oven to 400° F. In food grinder, with fine blade, grind 1¼ cups of the nuts, a few at a time, till you have 1½ cups, ground. Add 3 tablespoons sugar; mix well. With back of spoon, press this nut mixture to bottom and up sides of 8-inch or 9-inch pie plate, forming ¼-inch edge around rim. Bake 6 to 8 minutes or until light brown; cool.

2

In double boiler, combine gelatin, ¼ cup sugar and salt. Stir in egg yolks *well,* then *slowly* stir in scalded milk. Cook over simmering water, stirring constantly, until mixture coats metal spoon. Remove from heat. Let cool; chill till filling mounds when dropped from spoon.

3

Beat filling smooth with egg beater; add cherries and rum. Beat egg whites till soft peaks form; gradually add ¼ cup sugar, while beating until stiff. Fold into filling.

4

Pour all but 1 cup of filling into cooled nut crust; refrigerate pie and reserved filling. As soon as reserved filling mounds when dropped from spoon, heap it on center of pie; chill 4 hours. Meanwhile, soak ¼ cup Brazil-nut meats in boiling water.

5

At serving time: Whip cream; sweeten, if desired; spoon around top outer edge of pie. Over pie, with sharp paring knife, shave ¼ cup soaked Brazil-nut meats. Makes 8 servings.

*About 1 pound Brazil nuts in the shell.

desserts

Almost everyone loves desserts, and these are desserts to dream of. Fabulously rich or refreshingly light, each provides a memorable ending to a meal

A spectacular without equal,
crêpes suzettes can be made hours ahead of their flaming finale

---

CRÊPES SUZETTES

---

2 eggs
½ cup sifted all-purpose flour
1 tablespoon salad oil
¼ teaspoon salt
1 teaspoon granulated sugar
⅔ cup milk
6 sugar cubes

1 orange
¼ cup orange juice
¼ cup butter or margarine
¼ cup Curaçao or Cointreau
    orange twists
¼ cup Grand Marnier (or
    brandy)

1

Day before or early in day: In medium bowl, beat eggs until frothy; beat in flour till blended, then oil, salt, sugar, milk until smooth.

2

Lightly grease small skillet, about 5 to 6 inches across, then heat it till a drop of water sizzles in it. Pour about 2 tablespoons of batter in skillet, then quickly rotate skillet so as to cover bottom with batter; cook, turning once, until lightly browned on both sides. Remove from pan and repeat with rest of batter, making and stacking at least 10 crêpes. Wrap them well in foil or plastic wrap; refrigerate.

3

Rub sugar cubes over orange to absorb some oil from peel. In small saucepan, combine these cubes with orange juice, butter and Curaçao. Heat till butter melts and sugar is dissolved. Pour into bowl; cover; refrigerate.

4

About 5 minutes before serving: In crêpe pan or chafing dish over medium heat, reheat orange sauce. Fold crêpes in quarters; place in sauce to reheat, spooning on sauce. Add twist of orange, then take to table in darkened room.

5

With crêpe pan over small flame, pour Grand Marnier gently over sauce. Heat, without stirring, but do not boil. Then ignite with long match. When flame dies, serve crêpes and sauce. Makes 4 or 5 servings.

CRÊPES SUZETTES

GERMAN DESSERT PANCAKE

L ike a soufflé, this is a dessert
to be served, all puffy and golden, the very minute it's done

---

GERMAN DESSERT PANCAKE

⅓ cup sifted all-purpose flour
¼ teaspoon baking powder
⅓ cup milk
2 eggs, slightly beaten

2 tablespoons butter or margarine
1 tablespoon confectioners' sugar
4 lemon wedges

1

About 25 minutes before serving: Preheat oven to 425° F. In small bowl, combine flour and baking powder. Beat in milk and eggs, leaving batter a bit lumpy.

2

In 10-inch skillet with heatproof handle, melt butter. When butter is very hot, pour in batter, all at once. Bake 15 to 18 minutes until pancake is golden. Sprinkle with sugar. Serve hot with lemon wedges to squeeze over pancakes. Makes 4 servings.

SWEDISH PANCAKES

1 cup sifted all-purpose flour
2 tablespoons granulated sugar
½ teaspoon salt
3 eggs, slightly beaten
3 cups milk

melted butter or margarine
few drops vanilla extract
lingonberry preserves
sweetened whipped cream
(optional)

1

About 2 hours before serving: Sift flour with sugar and salt. In large bowl, combine eggs, milk, 2 tablespoons melted butter and vanilla; beat just until well blended. Add flour mixture, all at once; blend well; refrigerate.

2

At serving time: Start heating plätt pan; brush with butter. (If you don't have plätt pan, fold 3-inch-wide strips of foil lengthwise in half twice; form into about seven 3-inch circles, fastening ends together with paper clips or staples. Set on greased heated griddle.)

3

Remove batter from refrigerator; beat slightly. When plätt pan is very hot, pour 1 tablespoon batter into each section (or into each foil circle); cook until top is covered with tiny bubbles, underside well browned. Turn each pancake; brown other side; keep warm; make rest of pancakes.

4

Allow 7 or 8 pancakes for each serving. Pass lingonberry preserves and cream. Makes 10 servings.

ZABAGLIONE

3 egg yolks
¾ cup granulated sugar
2 teaspoons grated lemon peel

5 teaspoons lemon juice
½ cup sherry or Marsala wine

1

About 30 minutes before serving: In double boiler, beat egg yolks slightly. Add sugar and rest of ingredients. Cook over boiling water, beating constantly with rotary beater, until thick and fluffy as whipped cream. Remove from water. Serve hot. Makes 4 servings.

TOASTED SNOW SQUARES

1 envelope unflavored gelatin
granulated sugar
1¼ cups boiling water
3 egg whites, unbeaten
¼ teaspoon salt
1 teaspoon vanilla extract
2 egg yolks

⅓ cup melted butter
1 tablespoon grated lemon peel
2 tablespoons lemon juice
⅓ cup heavy or whipping cream,
   whipped
crumbs from 16 graham crackers
   (1 cup)

1

Several hours ahead: In small bowl, blend gelatin with ⅔ cup sugar. Add boiling water, while stirring, until dissolved; cool slightly. In large bowl, place egg whites, salt and vanilla. Add gelatin mixture; with electric mixer at high speed, beat until mixture has consistency of thick cream. Turn into 9″ by 9″ by 2″ pan; refrigerate until firm.

2

About 1 hour before serving: In small bowl, beat egg yolks until thick and lemon-colored. Gradually add ⅓ cup sugar, continuing to beat. Blend in melted butter, lemon peel and juice; fold in whipped cream; refrigerate.

3

At serving time: Cut gelatin mixture into 1-inch squares; roll each in cracker crumbs. Heap in sherbet glasses; top with sauce. Makes 8 servings.

Use your very best crystal bowl to show off this gorgeous party desert—layers of creamy custard alternating with a port-wine-and-raspberry gelatin

JEWELED BAVARIAN

2 3-ounce packages raspberry-
   flavor gelatin
2 cups hot water
2 cups port
1 envelope unflavored gelatin
dash salt

granulated sugar
2 eggs, separated
1¼ cups milk, scalded
1¾ cups heavy or whipping
   cream
1 teaspoon vanilla extract

1

Early in the day: To raspberry gelatin in small bowl, add hot water; stir till gelatin is dissolved. Stir in port. Pour 1 cup of mixture into 9″ by 5″

by 3″ pan; chill. (Also, in bowl, chill remaining mixture.)

2

In double boiler, combine unflavored gelatin, salt and 2 tablespoons sugar. Stir in beaten egg yolks well; stir in scalded milk slowly. Cook over simmering water, stirring constantly, until custard just coats a metal spoon. Remove at once; refrigerate, stirring occasionally, until both it and gelatin mixture in bowl just mound when dropped from spoon. (To hasten mounding, you may set mixtures in bowls of ice and water; then stir constantly.)

3

Whip 1 cup of the cream; add vanilla; refrigerate. When custard mounds (if it's too stiff, beat with rotary beater), beat egg whites to soft peaks; then gradually beat in ¼ cup sugar until stiff. Fold into custard with whipped cream.

4

In 2-quart crystal bowl, alternate layers of Bavarian and gelatin mixtures, both of mounding consistency. Refrigerate.

5

At dessert time: Cut pan of firm port jelly into ½-inch cubes. Whip ¾ cup cream; spoon onto Bavarian; sprinkle with port cubes. Carry to buffet; guests serve themselves in sherbet glasses. Makes 12 servings.

Here a few additions turn fruit-flavored gelatin, an everyday treat, into a triumph

---

CHERRY-SHERRY JUBILEE

1 17-ounce can pitted, dark sweet cherries
1 3-ounce cherry-flavor gelatin dessert
½ cup sherry
⅓ cup slivered toasted almonds
whipped cream for garnish

1

Early in day: Drain cherries. Add enough water to cherry syrup to make 1¾ cups. In saucepan, bring syrup to simmering point. Pour over gelatin; stir until dissolved. Add cherries, sherry, almonds. Chill.

2

At serving time: With a fork, break up gelatin mixture; spoon into sherbet glasses. Top with whipped cream. Makes 6 servings.

Sweet yet tart, the cranberry topping sets off the rich filling to the peak of perfection

---

CRANBERRY CHEESECAKE

1 cup packaged cornflake
crumbs
granulated sugar
½ teaspoon ground cinnamon
3 tablespoons melted butter or
margarine
2 16-ounce containers creamed
cottage cheese

4 eggs, unbeaten
¼ cup all-purpose flour
½ cup heavy or whipping cream
1 tablespoon lemon juice
1 tablespoon vanilla extract
2 cups fresh or frozen whole
cranberries
1½ teaspoons unflavored gelatin

1

Day before: In small bowl, thoroughly combine cornflake crumbs, ¼ cup granulated sugar, cinnamon and melted butter. Use to cover bottom of 9-inch springform pan, packing firmly. Preheat oven to 350° F.

2

Into large bowl, with spoon, press cottage cheese through fine sieve. With electric mixer at high speed, beat in eggs, one at a time, beating well after each addition. Thoroughly beat in flour and 1 cup granulated sugar. Beat in cream, lemon juice and vanilla, continuing to beat until very well blended.

3

Pour cheese mixture into crumb-lined pan; bake 50 minutes. Turn off oven and allow cheesecake to set for 30 minutes longer. Remove from oven to rack to cool. Refrigerate.

4

About 4 hours before serving: In saucepan, combine cranberries, ¾ cup water and 1 cup sugar. Cook this mixture 5 minutes or until skins pop, stirring occasionally. Meanwhile, soften gelatin in 2 tablespoons water, and stir it into hot cranberries until dissolved. Refrigerate mixture until it just begins to thicken. Next, gently loosen cheesecake from sides of pan with spatula and carefully remove sides. Loosen cheesecake from bottom of pan and slowly slide onto serving plate.

5

Gently pour cranberry mixture onto cheesecake, spreading it over top. Refrigerate cake until topping is set—about 3 hours. Makes 16 servings.

For those who prefer a fine-grained cheesecake that is made with cream cheese rather than cottage, here's a tender, light, orange-scented version

---

DELUXE CHEESECAKE

---

1 cup sifted all-purpose flour
granulated sugar
grated lemon peel
vanilla extract
½ cup butter or margarine,
 softened
3 egg yolks

5 8-ounce packages cream
 cheese, softened
½ teaspoon grated orange peel
3 tablespoons flour
¼ teaspoon salt
5 medium eggs
¼ cup heavy or whipping cream

1

Day before serving: In medium bowl, mix 1 cup flour, ¼ cup sugar, 1 teaspoon grated lemon peel, ¼ teaspoon vanilla. With pastry blender or 2 knives used scissor-fashion, cut in butter and 1 egg yolk. Shape into ball; wrap in waxed paper; refrigerate 1 hour.

2

Preheat oven to 400° F. Between pieces of floured waxed paper, roll about one-third of dough into 9½-inch circle. Place on bottom of 9-inch springform pan; trim to fit. Bake 10 minutes, or until golden; cool.

3

Grease side of springform pan; fit over pastry-lined base. Roll rest of dough into 15″ by 4″ rectangle; cut in half lengthwise; use to line side of pan, patching if necessary. Raise oven heat to 500° F.

4

With electric mixer at low speed, beat cheese until fluffy. Combine 1¾ cups sugar with ¼ teaspoon vanilla, orange peel, 3 tablespoons flour, salt, ½ teaspoon lemon peel; slowly add to cheese, beating until smooth. Add eggs and 2 yolks, one at a time, beating after each addition. Stir in cream. Turn into pastry-lined pan. Bake at 500° F. 12 minutes or until dough is golden. Lower oven heat to 200° F.; bake 1 hour (cake may crack). Cool on rack away from drafts. Remove side of pan; refrigerate cake for 24 hours, if possible. Makes 12 servings.

Ways to serve: Sprinkle cake with chopped, toasted nuts. Or cover with ¼-inch layer of sour cream; refrigerate. Or spread strawberry, peach, apricot, or cherry jam or preserves on top of cooled cake.

A classic of the French cuisine, this recipe results in a memorable dessert worth every bit of the time and tender loving care required to produce it

BABA AU RHUM

4 cups all-purpose flour
¼ cup granulated sugar
1 teaspoon salt
2 packages active dry yeast
¾ cup butter or margarine
6 eggs
⅔ cup cut-up citron or currants

Rum Sauce (below)
⅓ cup apricot jam
2 tablespoons lemon juice
1 cup each: honeydew and
 cantaloupe chunks,
 strawberries and grapes
whipped cream

1

At least 6 hours before serving: In large bowl, combine 2 cups flour, sugar, salt and yeast. In medium saucepan, heat ½ cup water and butter until very warm (120° to 130° F.) . Butter does not have to melt.

2

With electric mixer at medium speed, gradually add liquid to dry ingredients. Beat 2 minutes, scraping bowl occasionally. Add eggs, one at a time, beating well after each. Add citron and enough flour (about 1 cup) to make thick batter; beat 2 minutes at high speed, scraping bowl occasionally. With spoon, stir in 1 cup flour; stir until dough is smooth. Cover with towel; let rise in warm place (80° to 85° F.) away from draft until almost doubled, about 1 hour.

3

With spoon, stir down dough; turn into greased 12-cup ring mold or 10-inch tube pan and spread evenly. Cover with towel and let rise in warm place (80° to 85° F.) until tripled and almost to top of pan. Preheat oven to 375° F. Bake 40 to 45 minutes or until golden. Remove from pan; cool on rack. Meanwhile, make Rum Sauce. Set cooled baba on platter; spoon on Rum Sauce, let stand 2 hours, occasionally spooning on sauce from platter.

4

Just before serving, press apricot jam through strainer and combine with lemon juice; brush over top and sides of baba. Fill center with fruit. Serve with whipped cream. Makes twenty-eight 1-inch slices.

RUM SAUCE: In small saucepan, simmer 1½ cups granulated sugar, 2 cups water, 4 thin orange and lemon slices for about 5 minutes; cool. Add ½ to 1 cup of white rum. Makes about 3 cups.

BABA AU RHUM

T he Ritz-Carlton Hotel, in New York City, is gone, but not its famed specialty, a snowy dessert with a sauce that seems blended of cream and sunshine

---

EGGS À LA NEIGE

---

4 cups milk
6 eggs, separated
granulated sugar
salt
1½ cups heavy or whipping
  cream

¾ teaspoon vanilla extract
1½ tablespoons flour
2 pints fresh strawberries,
  sliced
1 square unsweetened chocolate

1

Day before or early in day: In large skillet, scald milk. Meanwhile, beat egg whites until frothy; gradually add ¾ cup sugar, ¼ teaspoon salt, beating until stiff. Onto hot milk, drop three large mounds of meringue, 1 inch apart; cook 5 minutes, turning once with slotted spoon; drain on paper towel. Repeat; cover; refrigerate. Reserve milk.

2

In double boiler, scald cream with vanilla and 1½ cups reserved milk. Beat egg yolks until light; beat in ½ cup sugar, dash salt, flour, a little of cream-milk mixture; stir this back into the mixture in double boiler; cook over hot, *not boiling,* water, stirring, until sauce coats metal spoon. Cover; refrigerate.

3

About 20 minutes before serving: Place strawberries in deep serving dish. Over them, heap the chilled meringues; pour on custard sauce. With vegetable peeler, shave some chocolate on top. Makes 8 servings.

CARAMEL-CUSTARD MOLD

---

granulated sugar
6½ cups milk
9 eggs
5 egg yolks

¾ teaspoon salt
2 teaspoons almond extract
¾ cup heavy or whipping cream,
  whipped

1

Day before: In heavy 10-inch skillet, place 1 cup sugar; shake so sugar is level. Place over high heat and watch for sugar to begin melting. Then immediately tilt pan back and forth slowly to keep sugar moving.

By the time sugar has completely melted, it will be light golden brown. Remove from heat at once, and carefully pour into bottom of 2½-quart heatproof soufflé dish. Preheat oven to 325° F.

2

In 6-quart kettle, scald milk. Meanwhile, place eggs and egg yolks in large bowl; add ½ cup sugar; with electric mixer at medium speed, beat until completely blended.

3

Pour eggs, all at once, stirring constantly, into scalded milk; add salt and almond extract. Pour custard into soufflé dish; set in pan; place on oven rack; fill pan with boiling water to within ½ inch of top. Bake 1 hour and 20 minutes, or until knife inserted in center comes out clean. Remove soufflé dish from water; cool slightly on rack. Refrigerate.

4

At serving time: Run small spatula all around custard. Invert on rimmed serving plate (caramel will collect around custard). Spoon ¼ cup caramel syrup from around custard; fold into cream; pass. Makes 12 servings.

CRÈME BRÛLÉE

6 egg yolks
6 tablespoons granulated sugar
3 cups heavy cream, scalded

1 teaspoon vanilla extract
½ cup packed light brown sugar

1

Day before or early in day: In double boiler, with rotary beater, beat yolks and granulated sugar until blended; slowly stir in scalded cream. Cook over hot, *not boiling,* water, stirring constantly, until slightly thickened. Add vanilla; pour custard into 1½-quart shallow glass baking dish; refrigerate.

2

Several hours before serving: Preheat broiler, with rack removed, if manufacturer directs. Carefully sift brown sugar over top of custard; set it on broiler rack, 3 inches from heat; broil about 4 minutes or until sugar melts, making a shiny caramel top. Refrigerate.

3

To serve: Set brûlée on tray; surround with fruits if desired. Makes 6 servings.

A thrifty way to use up left-over cake, trifle can also be a dessert in the grand manner. As it is here, garnished with glacéed cherries and cream

PINWHEEL TRIFLE

4½ cups milk
 ½ cup granulated sugar
dash salt
 6 eggs
 1 teaspoon vanilla extract
12 to 15 slices baker's or

homemade jelly-roll, each
 ½-inch thick
 ½ cup sherry
 9 glacéed cherries
angelica (optional)
 ¼ cup heavy or whipping cream

1

Day before serving: In double boiler, scald 4 cups of the milk; add sugar and salt, then place over hot water.

2

Beat eggs well, add ½ cup milk; slowly stir into scalded-milk mixture. Cook, over simmering water, stirring, for 10 minutes until custard coats spoon. Turn into large bowl; cover with waxed paper; chill.

3

About 1 hour before serving: Into custard, stir vanilla; turn into 10-cup deep oval serving dish; refrigerate. Lay jelly-roll slices on pastry board;

sprinkle with half of sherry; arrange, sherry side down, on custard; sprinkle with rest of sherry; refrigerate.

4

Just before serving: In spaces between jelly-roll slices, place glacéed cherries, with 2 angelica leaves tucked beside each. Whip cream stiff; with decorating bag and tube number 30, use to make stars between slices as pictured.

5

Serve jelly-roll slice with some custard spooned over it. Makes 12 to 15 servings.

Simple and simply delicious— individual custards that are velvet-smooth on the tongue

---

BAKED CUSTARDS

---

4 eggs
¼ cup granulated sugar
¼ teaspoon salt
2 to 2½ cups milk or milk and

cream
1 teaspoon vanilla extract
nutmeg or flaked coconut

1

Early in day: Preheat oven to 300° F. Butter 5 or 6 custard cups.

2

Into large bowl, break eggs; with electric mixer at medium speed, or rotary beater, beat until fluffy. Add sugar, salt; beat until thick and lemon-colored. Add milk, vanilla; beat again until thoroughly combined.

3

Pour mixture through fine strainer into custard cups, filling each to about ½ inch from top; top with nutmeg or coconut. Set custard cups in shallow baking pan; place on oven rack. Fill pan with hot water to ¾ inch from top of cups. Bake about 1 hour. Near end of baking time, insert knife in center of custard. When knife comes out clean, custards are done. Remove at once from oven; remove from water; let cool on rack. Refrigerate.

4

Serve right in custard cups. Or run spatula all around inside of each cup; unmold onto dessert plates. Makes 5 or 6 servings.

KITCHENETTE CARAMEL PUDDING

1 cup packed dark brown sugar
3 slices fresh white or raisin
  bread, buttered, cut into ½-
  inch squares
3 eggs

1 cup milk
dash salt
½ teaspoon vanilla extract
vanilla ice cream or whipped
  cream

1

About 2 hours before serving: Generously butter inside of double-boiler top; pour in brown sugar; add bread squares.

2

Beat eggs with milk, salt and vanilla; pour over bread; do not stir. Cook, over boiling water, covered, 1 hour. Serve warm, with ice cream or whipped cream. Makes 4 servings.

With deep-South expansiveness, this dessert layers orange sections and coconut with a sherry-flavored sauce made of egg yolks, sugar and cream

SOUTHERN AMBROSIA

1 cup milk
1 cup heavy cream
4 egg yolks
¼ cup granulated sugar
1 tablespoon flour

¼ teaspoon salt
3 tablespoons sherry
8 medium oranges, sectioned
1½ cups grated fresh coconut;
  or 1 can flaked coconut

1

Early in day: In double boiler, heat milk with cream until tiny bubbles appear around edge.

In medium bowl, beat egg yolks slightly with fork; stir in sugar, flour, salt. Add hot milk mixture slowly, stirring constantly. Return mixture to double-boiler; cook over hot, *not boiling,* water, stirring, until slightly thickened. Cool. Add sherry. Cover; refrigerate. Makes 2 cups.

2

To serve: In individual dishes, make layer of custard sauce, then of well-drained orange sections, then of coconut; repeat. Makes 8 servings.

CHARLOTTE RUSSE

2 envelopes unflavored gelatin
¾ cup granulated sugar
¼ teaspoon salt
4 eggs, separated
2 cups milk, scalded

⅓ cup brandy
9 ladyfingers, split
2 cups heavy or whipping cream
9 maraschino cherries for
   garnish

1

Early in day: In double boiler, combine gelatin, sugar, salt. Stir in egg yolks; slowly stir in milk. Cook mixture over hot, *not boiling*, water, stirring, until it coats spoon. Cool. Add 3 tablespoons of the brandy. Refrigerate until mixture mounds slightly.

2

Sprinkle remaining brandy on ladyfingers; use to line side of 2-quart fluted tube mold or 3½-inch deep 9-inch tube pan.

3

In large bowl, beat egg whites until stiff but not dry. Whip cream. Fold gelatin mixture into egg whites; fold in whipped cream. Turn into mold. Refrigerate until firm.

4

To serve: Unmold onto serving platter. If desired, garnish with more whipped cream and maraschino cherries. Makes 12 servings.

n instant dessert, yet one worthy of its imperial name—ice cream topped with strawberries that have been marinated in brandy and Cointreau

STRAWBERRIES ROMANOFF

1 quart strawberries, cleaned
   and hulled
2 tablespoons brandy
2 tablespoons Cointreau or

Curaçao
½ pint vanilla ice cream
½ cup heavy or whipping cream,
   whipped

1

About 10 minutes before serving: In well chilled bowl, marinate strawberries in brandy and Cointreau or Curaçao, or all three.

2

In chilled bowl, stir ice cream till softened; top with cream; fold in berries; ladle into sherbet dishes. Makes 6 servings.

GALA PEAR PYRAMID

½ cup granulated sugar
2 tablespoons lemon juice
2 tablespoons butter or

margarine
12 fresh pears, pared, stems left on
orange peel, slivered

1

Early in day: Preheat oven to 350° F. In saucepan, simmer sugar with lemon juice, butter and 1 cup water 5 minutes. In large roasting pan, arrange pears; pour lemon syrup over them. Bake, covered, 50 to 60 minutes, or until pears are fork-tender; remove from syrup; cover pears and syrup; refrigerate.

2

At serving time: In shallow bowl or compote, arrange pears in pyramid; skim syrup; pour over pears. Garnish with orange peel. Makes 12 servings.

A splendidly lavish dessert that people who watch calories—and everyone else too—will enjoy

FRUIT MÉLANGE

2 cups cranberry juice
¼ cup granulated sugar
1 cup ginger ale
2 cups halved seedless grapes
2 cups pared, sliced apples
2 cups halved strawberries
2 cups drained, canned or
fresh grapefruit sections

2 cups drained, canned or frozen
sliced peaches
2 cups drained, canned pineapple
chunks
1 cup sour cream
crystalized ginger, coarsely
chopped
mint sprigs for garnish

1

Early in day: In medium bowl, combine cranberry juice, sugar and ginger ale. In 12-cup punch bowl, layer evenly grapes, apples, strawberries, grapefruit sections, sliced peaches and pineapple.

2

Pour cranberry-juice mixture over fruit, retaining layers; refrigerate several hours.

3

At serving time: Heap sour cream on top of fruit, then sprinkle with ginger. If desired, add a few mint sprigs. Makes 12 servings.

SNOWY ORANGE CUPS

4 large oranges
2 pints orange sherbet,
    slightly softened
1 pint fresh strawberries

granulated sugar
light rum (optional)
canned, flaked or grated fresh
    coconut

1

Day before serving: Slice top from each orange about one-third of the way down. With sharp knife, cut out all orange sections, reserving them for later use. Then, if desired, make pretty, saw-toothed pattern around top edge of each orange shell.

2

Fill each orange shell with sherbet, pressing it down into shell so it fills saw-toothed edge and rounding it high in center. Set orange cups, side by side, in shallow pan; place in freezer. Freeze.

3

Early in day: Wash strawberries; reserve 12 for garnishing. Cut remaining strawberries into small pieces; add sugar to taste; sprinkle with rum, if desired. Refrigerate until needed, stirring occasionally.

4

About 15 minutes before serving: With teaspoon, make small cavity down through center of sherbet in each orange cup. Fill with cut strawberries; sprinkle top generously with coconut; serve at once. Makes 4 servings.

COCOA-CREAM RING

1 4-ounce bar German's sweet
    cooking chocolate
1 cup broken walnuts
2½ cups packaged cocoa-flavored

rice or corn cereal
10 vanilla ice-cream balls
    bottled chocolate-caramel sauce

1

About 30 minutes before serving: Refrigerate 1¼-quart ring mold. In double boiler, over warm, *not hot,* water, melt chocolate. Add walnuts and cereal. Toss until uniformly coated with chocolate. Press lightly into ring mold. Refrigerate 25 minutes; unmold on serving dish. Heap ice-cream balls in center; drizzle on sauce. Makes 6 servings.

NAPOLEONS

Delectable enough to be any Emperor's favorite, napoleons, in fact, take their name not from the famous French general but from the city of Naples

---

NAPOLEONS

4½ cups all-purpose flour
1 pound butter, chilled
1 tablespoon vinegar
2 3¼-ounce packages vanilla
  pudding-and-pie-filling mix
1 envelope unflavored gelatin

2 cups heavy or whipping cream
1 teaspoon vanilla extract
1 cup confectioners' sugar
¼ cup semisweet-chocolate pieces
1 teaspoon light corn syrup

1

Several days before serving: In large bowl, combine flour and ½ pound of the butter in small pieces (refrigerate rest of butter). With pastry blender or two knives used scissor-fashion, cut in butter, until mixture is like cornmeal. Mix 1 cup cold water with vinegar; pour over flour mixture. With fork, mix well; shape into ball; wrap. Refrigerate ½ hour. On floured surface, roll pastry into rectangle ¼ inch thick.

Starting at narrow end of dough, dot two thirds of it with remaining chilled ½ pound butter. Fold unbuttered third over center third, then fold last third on top, making 3 layers. Fold opposite ends so they completely overlap each other, making equal thirds and a block shape with straight sides. Wrap in foil; refrigerate ½ hour. Reroll dough and repeat folding, wrapping and refrigerating three more times. Refrigerate dough overnight or for several days.

3

Early in day: Remove dough from refrigerator; let rest ½ hour; divide dough into 6 equal parts. Preheat oven to 425° F. On floured surface, roll one of sixths of dough into 14″ by 12″ rectangle. Fold in half; on large ungreased cookie sheet, unfold. Prick top generously with fork. Bake 10 minutes or until golden brown. Carefully remove to flat surface; cool. Repeat rolling with remaining 5 portions of dough, baking 1 sheet at a time and making six 14″ by 12″ pastry rectangles in all. (Refrigerate dough if it gets too soft.)

4

To make filling: Cook pie-filling mix as label directs, but use 3 cups milk. Pour into large bowl; cover with waxed paper; refrigerate until completely chilled. Onto 3 tablespoons water, in measuring cup, sprinkle unflavored gelatin; stir over hot water until completely dissolved; cool slightly. Whip cream with vanilla until just starting to mound; gradually add cooled gelatin while continuing to beat cream stiff. Fold whipped-cream mixture into chilled pudding; refrigerate. Makes enough filling for 18 napoleons.

5

In small bowl, combine confectioners' sugar with about 1½ tablespoons water until smooth. Over warm water, melt chocolate with corn syrup; stir in 1 teaspoon water for glaze. Place in decorator bag with tube no. 2. Generously frost top of one pastry rectangle with white icing; with chocolate glaze, make crosswise lines, 1 inch apart, from one side to the other. While icing is wet, draw tip of knife lengthwise through icing and chocolate crosslines, drawing lines 1 inch apart, at opposite ends of rectangle to form zigzag design.

Spread custard filling over 2 of the rectangles; stack them; top with decorated pastry rectangle; refrigerate at least 1 hour. With sharp knife, trim off uneven ends. Cut in thirds crosswise. Cut into 18 napoleons.

Note: Freezer-wrap and freeze 3 baked pastry rectangles for later use. Thaw; fill and frost as above.

P

uffy, high and golden, perfect
cream puffs are not hard to make if you follow this recipe

CREAM PUFFS

½ cup butter or margarine   1 cup sifted all-purpose flour
1 cup boiling water   4 eggs, unbeaten
½ teaspoon salt   Cream-Puff Filling (opposite)

1

Early in day: Preheat oven to 400° F. In medium saucepan, heat butter with boiling water, stirring occasionally, until butter is melted. Turn heat low; add salt and flour, both at once, and stir vigorously, until mixture leaves sides of pan in smooth compact ball.

2

Immediately remove from heat. Quickly add eggs, one at a time, beating with spoon until smooth after each addition. After last egg has been added, beat until mixture has satinlike sheen. Drop mixture by table-spoonfuls, 3 inches apart, on greased cookie sheet, shaping into eight mounds that point up in center. Bake 50 minutes—Cream Puffs should be puffed high and golden. Remove to rack; cool.

3

To serve: Split Cream Puffs almost all the way around. Or slice off top of each. Fill with Cream-Puff Filling, ice cream, or sweetened whipped cream, flavored with almond, vanilla or rum extract. Set tops back on. Nice served with confectioners' sugar; crushed, sweetened berries; or sliced peaches. Makes 8 puffs.

CHOCOLATE ECLAIRS: Preheat oven to 400° F. Make cream-puff mixture (above). Drop 8 rounded tablespoons, about 2 inches apart, in rows 6 inches apart, onto ungreased baking sheet. Now, working carefully with small spatula, spread each ball of dough into 4″ by 1″ rectangle, rounding sides and piling dough on top. Bake 40 minutes or until golden. When done, cool on rack.

To serve: Make lengthwise slit in side of each; fill with Cream-Puff Filling or whipped cream; top with Thin Chocolate Glaze. In double boiler over hot, *not boiling,* water, melt 2 tablespoons butter or margarine with 2 squares unsweetened chocolate and 2 tablespoons hot water. Remove from heat. Blend in 1 to 1½ cups sifted confectioners' sugar. Beat till smooth, but not stiff. Spread over eclairs.

CREAM-PUFF FILLING

⅔ cup granulated sugar
¼ cup flour
¼ teaspoon salt
2 eggs, slightly beaten

¾ cup scalded milk
1 teaspoon vanilla extract
½ cup heavy or whipping cream, whipped

1

Early in day: In double boiler, mix sugar, flour, salt, eggs, then milk; blend thoroughly. Cook over boiling water, stirring constantly, 5 minutes. Cook, stirring occasionally, 5 minutes more. Chill. Add vanilla; fold in cream. Fills 8 cream puffs.

Y ou "forget" this torte by leaving it in a turned-off oven overnight. When served the next day, with fruit and whipped cream, it's *un*forgettable

FORGOTTEN TORTE

6 egg whites, at room
   temperature
¼ teaspoon salt
½ teaspoon cream of tartar
1½ cups granulated sugar

1 teaspoon vanilla extract
⅛ teaspoon almond extract
1 cup heavy or whipping
   cream, whipped
sweetened berries or other fruit

1

About 1 hour before overnight "baking": Butter bottom, not sides, of 9-inch tube pan. In large bowl, place egg whites, salt and cream of tartar. Preheat oven to 450° F. With electric mixer at medium speed, beat until foamy; gradually add sugar, 2 tablespoons at a time, beating well after each addition. Add extracts; continue beating until meringue makes stiff, glossy peaks.

2

Spread evenly in tube pan. Place in oven. Turn off heat at once. Let stand in oven overnight. Next morning, loosen edge of torte with sharp knife. Turn onto serving plate; let stand until needed.

3

To serve: Frost torte with whipped cream; top with fruit; serve in wedges. Makes 10 servings.

Decorated with whipped cream

and glazed walnuts, this latticed, double-ring torte is almost too pretty to eat, but entirely too delicious not to

WALNUT MERINGUE TORTE

3 egg whites
1/4 teaspoon cream of tartar
granulated sugar

32 walnut halves
2 cups heavy or whipping cream
2 pints butter-pecan ice cream

1

Day before: Cut two 9-inch waxed-paper circles; place each on greased cookie sheet. Preheat oven to 300° F.

2

In medium bowl, with electric mixer at high speed, beat egg whites with cream of tartar until frothy. With mixer at low speed, beat in 1 cup sugar, 2 tablespoons at a time, until stiff. Continue beating at high speed, until very stiff and glossy.

3

With half of meringue mixture in decorating bag and pastry tube number 5, make ring around inner edge of one of waxed-paper circles. Then top entire circle, first with three parallel lines of meringue going in one direction, then three more, crisscrossing them. Repeat with other circle. Bake both meringue rings in same oven for 30 minutes, or until light brown, exchanging lower cookie sheet with upper one after 15 minutes. When done, peel waxed paper from meringues at once and place meringues on cake racks. Cool; cover with waxed paper.

4

In small skillet over medium heat, melt 1/2 cup sugar until it forms golden syrup. Drop walnuts, a few at a time, into syrup, coating all sides. With fork, place two walnut halves together, lifting carefully to greased cookie sheet to dry; repeat; let stand at room temperature.

5

About 15 minutes before serving: Whip cream until stiff. On large cake plate, spread thin layer of whipped cream in circle of same size as one of meringue rings. Over it place one of meringue rings. Now spoon ice cream evenly over this ring, all the way out to edges, then top with second meringue ring. With some of remaining whipped cream in decorating bag and pastry tube number 5, fill each of the 16 holes in the lattice pattern with a swirling mound; top each with glazed walnut. Make whipped-cream rosettes around sides. Makes 12 servings.

MOUSSE AU CHOCOLAT

1 6-ounce package semisweet-
  chocolate pieces
6 egg yolks

2 teaspoons vanilla extract
6 egg whites
1 square unsweetened chocolate

1

Early in day: In double boiler, over hot, *not boiling*, water, melt chocolate pieces; remove from heat. With spoon, beat in yolks and vanilla.

2

Beat egg whites until stiff, but not dry; fold into chocolate mixture. Spoon into 8 to 10 demitasse cups. Refrigerate 4 hours, or until served.

3

With vegetable peeler or small paring knife, shave off curls from unsweetened chocolate. Serve each mousse topped wtih curls. Makes 8 to 10 servings.

n Italian delicacy, tortoni is served in the tiny paper cups in which it is frozen. Semisweet chocolate and toasted almonds enhance this version

CHOCO-NUT TORTONI

1 egg white
4 tablespoons granulated sugar
1 cup heavy or whipping cream
1 teaspoon vanilla extract
½ 6-ounce package semisweet-

chocolate pieces (½ cup)
1 teaspoon shortening
¼ cup canned toasted almonds,
  finely chopped

1

Early in day: Beat egg white until fairly stiff; gradually add 2 tablespoons of the sugar, beating until stiff. Whip cream; combine with 2 tablespoons sugar, vanilla; fold into beaten egg white. Turn into ice-cube tray; freeze until frozen ½ inch in from edges of tray. Melt chocolate with shortening over hot, *not boiling*, water. Turn frozen mixture into chilled bowl; stir until smooth but not melted; quickly fold in melted chocolate, then almonds. Turn into eight 2-ounce paper cups; freeze until just firm. Makes 8 servings.

Twelve splendid cookie-like layers, put together with whipped cream and topped with more cream (chocolate-flavored), glacéed cherries, walnuts

CHOCOLATE-CINNAMON TORTE

2¾ cups sifted all-purpose flour
2 tablespoons cinnamon
1½ cups butter
2 cups granulated sugar
2 eggs, unbeaten
1 square unsweetened chocolate

2 squares semisweet chocolate
4 cups heavy or whipping cream
2 tablespoons cocoa
12 glacéed cherries
12 walnut halves

1

Several days ahead: Preheat oven to 375° F. Grease two or three 9-inch layer-cake pans, line bottoms with waxed paper; grease again. Sift flour with cinnamon.

2

In large bowl, with mixer at medium speed, mix butter with sugar, then with eggs, until very light and fluffy. Then, at low speed, mix in flour mixture, a little at a time, until smooth.

3

With spatula, spread ⅓ cup "cookie" dough in very thin layer in each layer-cake pan; place in oven on two racks, making sure pans are not directly over one another. Bake about 8 to 12 minutes or until golden.

4

Immediately and carefully remove each "cookie" from pan to rack; cool. Continue baking "cookies" until all dough is used, making at least 12. Store, carefully stacked, in tight container.

5

About 1 hour before serving: Grate unsweetened chocolate medium fine; with vegetable peeler, shred semisweet chocolate into curls; whip cream. Place one "cookie" on cake plate; spread with ¼ to ⅓ cup whipped cream. Continue building the layers until you have 12-layer torte.

6

Fold cocoa and unsweetened chocolate into leftover whipped cream; heap over top of torte. Decorate top edge of torte with cherries and walnuts, then heap chocolate curls in center. Refrigerate about ½ hour before serving so that it will be easy to cut. Makes 12 wedges.

CHOCOLATE-CINNAMON TORTE

Concealed inside are extra strawberries to enhance the flavor of the strawberry ice cream

STRAWBERRY BAKED ALASKA

1 baked 9-inch yellow-cake layer	*strawberries, thawed, drained*
2 pints strawberry ice cream	*5 egg whites*
1 10-ounce package frozen sliced	*10 tablespoons granulated sugar*

1

Day before serving: Place cake layer on foil-covered cardboard circle.

2

Let ice cream soften slightly; pile in center of cake layer; make hollow in center top of ice cream. Fill with berries; freeze; cover with foil.

3

Several hours before serving: In large bowl, with electric mixer at high speed, beat egg whites until frothy; gradually sprinkle in sugar, 2 tablespoons at a time, beating until stiff peaks form when beater is raised.

4

With metal spatula, spread about two thirds of this meringue mixture over top and sides of Alaska. Put remaining meringue in decorating bag, and with number 3 tube in place, decorate top and sides of Alaska in any pattern desired. Return to freezer for at least 1 hour.

5

About 20 minutes before serving: Preheat oven to 500° F. With 2 wide spatulas, lift Alaska to cookie sheet; place in oven for about 2 or 3 minutes, or until meringue is just tinged with brown.

6

Remove from oven; with help of spatulas, place Alaska on serving plate. Let soften slightly, if necessary, then, with long-bladed sharp knife, cut into wedges. Makes 12 servings.

IGLOO: Use bakers' spongcake layer as base. Pile ice cream on top, leaving ½″ free around edge; omit berries. Cover with ½ recipe for meringue in step 3; bake as above.

BROWNIE: Use panful of uncut brownies as base. Top with brick ice cream; omit berries. Cover with ½ recipe for meringue as in step 3; bake as above.

ICE CREAM CLAD IN CHOCOLATE

4 cups fine chocolate wafer crumbs (2 8½-ounce packages)
1 cup butter or margarine, melted

2 pints each: vanilla, pistachio and chocolate ice cream, slightly softened

1

Anytime up to 2 weeks before serving: Prepare chocolate wafer crumbs in electric blender, or by rolling wafers with rolling pin. In medium bowl, combine crumbs with melted butter; set aside ⅔ cup crumb mixture. Firmly press remaining crumbs over bottom and up sides of 9-inch springform pan. Freeze about 15 minutes, or until firm. Quickly spread vanilla ice cream over bottom of springform pan in even layer; sprinkle with ⅓ cup reserved crumbs. Freeze until firm. Repeat with pistachio ice cream and chocolate ice cream, but omit sprinkling crumbs on chocolate layer. Cover pan with foil; Freeze.

2

About 10 minutes before serving: Unmold cake pan onto chilled serving plate. Garnish with coconut, if desired. Cut into wedges with knife dipped in cold water. Makes 12 servings.

Fabulously fresh-tasting, a sherbet that may be served either as a dessert, with lady fingers or poundcake, or as an accompaniment to the main course

FRESH CRANBERRY SHERBET

1 envelope unflavored gelatin
4 cups fresh cranberries

2 cups granulated sugar
⅓ cup lemon juice

1

Early in day: Sprinkle gelatin on ½ cup water to soften. In large saucepan, cook cranberries in 2½ cups water, covered, until skins pop open; force through sieve; add sugar and gelatin. Heat until gelatin dissolves; cool. Add lemon juice.

Turn into ice-cube tray; freeze until firm. Turn into chilled bowl; with electric mixer, beat until thick and mushy. Return mixture to tray; freeze until just firm enough to spoon out. Makes 4 to 6 dessert servings, or 8 small compotes with main course.

SHERBET-CREAM CAKE

A rainbow of an ice-cream cake, filled with raspberry, orange, and pistachio sherbets

SHERBET-CREAM CAKE

1½ pints raspberry sherbet
1½ pints orange sherbet
1½ pints pistachio ice cream
3 quarts vanilla ice cream
2 cups chopped pecans

2 cups shaved semisweet-chocolate squares, or coarsely chopped semisweet-chocolate pieces
1 pint heavy or whipping cream
green or red food color

1

Up to week ahead: With number 20 ice-cream scoop, make 8 balls from each of raspberry, orange and pistachio flavors. Place balls on chilled cookie sheet. Freeze very firm. Chill 10-inch tube pan.

2

In large bowl, with wooden spoon or electric mixer, beat 1½ quarts of the vanilla ice cream until softened and like heavy batter; stir in 1 cup chopped pecans and 1 cup shaved or chopped chocolate. Spoon enough of ice-cream mixture into chilled tube pan to make 1-inch layer. Quickly alternate half of raspberry, orange and pistachio balls on top of ice cream. Spoon rest of ice-cream mixture over balls; freeze.

3

Beat up remaining 1½ quarts vanilla ice cream as in step 2; add rest of pecans and chocolate. Continue alternating rest of raspberry, orange and pistachio balls, then cover with ice-cream mixture (cake pan will be full). Cover with foil; freeze.

4

Early in serving day: Remove tube pan from freezer. Run knife around outer and inner edges of pan. Quickly dip cake pan in and out of lukewarm water. Unmold ice cream on plate. Return to freezer.

5

2 hours before serving: Whip cream; tint a delicate green or pink; use to frost ice-cream cake; return to freezer.

6

About ½ hour before serving: Place ice-cream cake in refrigerator to soften. Use sharp knife dipped in hot water. Makes 12 servings.

A quite irresistible creaminess, coupled with the zest of fresh limes and lemons, has made this sherbet a prime favorite for thirty years and more

LIME MILK SHERBET

1 envelope unflavored gelatin	*2 tablespoons grated lime peel*
2 cups milk	*¼ cup lemon juice*
½ teaspoon salt	*½ cup lime juice*
1⅓ cups granulated sugar	*green food color*
2 cups light cream	

1

About 5 hours before serving: Sprinkle gelatin onto ½ cup of the milk in bowl; let soften 5 minutes. Set bowl over boiling water; stir until gelatin dissolves. Combine salt, sugar, remaining 1½ cups milk, cream, lime peel, lemon juice and lime juice; stir in gelatin; tint delicate green. (If mixture curdles, don't worry; curdling disappears during freezing.) Turn into ice-cube tray; freeze until frozen 1 inch in from edge of tray. Turn into chilled bowl; beat with rotary beater until smooth, but not melted. Return to tray; freeze just until firm. Makes 6 servings.

The pralines are made first, then crushed and whipped into this cool cloud of a soufflé. Serve it with sectioned tangerines and green grapes

---

PRALINE SOUFFLÉ SUPERB

1½ cups granulated sugar
½ teaspoon cream of tartar
1 cup blanched whole almonds
2 envelopes unflavored gelatin
⅔ cup boiling water

2 tablespoons rum
4 eggs, separated
1 cup milk
3¼ cups heavy or whipping cream

1

Day before or early in day: Butter cookie sheet well. In saucepan, combine sugar, cream of tartar, ½ cup cold water and almonds. Cook, without stirring, until dark molasses color, shaking pan occasionally; pour at once onto cookie sheet. Let cool and harden at room temperature.

2

Run spatula under praline to loosen it from cookie sheet; break some of it into electric-blender container; turn on high speed until powdered, then turn into bowl; repeat until all praline is powdered. (Or place in folded waxed paper and pound with hammer.)

3

Fold 30" by 12" piece of foil in half lengthwise; with cellophane tape, attach around rim of 1½-quart china soufflé dish to form collar.

4

Place gelatin in large mixing bowl; add boiling water, then beat with rotary beater until light and frothy. With same beater, beat in rum, egg yolks, milk and 3 cups powdered praline.

5

Beat egg whites until stiff, but not dry. Beat 3 cups of the cream; fold both into praline mixture. Carefully turn into prepared soufflé dish. Refrigerate 3 hours or longer.

6

Just before serving: Remove collar from soufflé dish. Place ¼ cup heavy cream, whipped, in decorating bag. With tube number 30, press out small half moons all around top outer edge of soufflé. Gently press remaining powdered praline all around sides of soufflé. Garnish with green grapes and sectioned tangerines, if desired. Makes 12 servings.

Τhe cold soufflé *par excellence,* elegant, delicious—and surprisingly easy to prepare

---

COLD SOUFFLÉ GRAND MARNIER

---

granulated sugar
Grand Marnier
2 tablespoons lemon juice
1 envelope, plus 2 teaspoons
   unflavored gelatin
7 eggs, separated

½ cup glacéed mixed fruits
½ cup canned, roasted, diced
   almonds
¼ teaspoon salt
2 cups heavy or whipping cream,
   whipped

1

Day before: In medium saucepan, mix ½ cup sugar, 1 cup water, ½ cup Grand Marnier, lemon juice and gelatin with egg yolks. Cook over medium heat, stirring, until mixture coats spoon and gelatin is dissolved. Pour into large bowl; refrigerate until like unbeaten egg white.

2

Meanwhile, soak finely cut-up glacéed fruits in 2 tablespoons Grand Marnier. Prepare foil collar for 7½-cup soufflé dish. Fold piece of foil 35″ by 12″ in half lengthwise; wrap around outside of soufflé dish, so that collar, 3 inches high, stands above rim; fasten with celophane tape. Lightly butter inside of foil collar. Into cooled gelatin mixture, fold in almonds and glacéed fruits.

3

Beat egg whites with salt until soft peaks form; gradually add ¼ cup sugar, beating until stiff. Fold cream and egg whites into gelatin mixture. Pour into prepared soufflé dish; refrigerate.

4

About 20 minutes before serving: Carefully remove foil collar. If desired, garnish with more whipped cream. Makes 10 servings.

COLD LEMON SOUFFLÉ

---

2 envelopes unflavored gelatin
8 eggs, separated
1 cup lemon juice
1 teaspoon salt

granulated sugar
2 teaspoon grated lemon peel
2 cups heavy or whipping cream,
   whipped

1

Early in day: Sprinkle gelatin over ½ cup cold water to soften.

In double boiler, combine egg yolks, lemon juice, salt and 1 cup sugar. Cook over boiling water, stirring constantly, until it coats back of spoon. Stir in gelatin and lemon peel; turn into 3-quart bowl; refrigerate until slightly thickened; stir occasionally. Meanwhile, prepare foil collar for 6-cup soufflé dish as in step 2 of Cold Soufflé Grand Marnier.

3

Beat egg whites until they hold their shape; gradually beat in 1 cup sugar; continue to beat until mixture holds peaks.

4

On top of lemon mixture, pile stiffly beaten egg whites and cream; gently fold mixture together. Pour into soufflé dish; refrigerate 3 hours or until firm but spongy. Makes 12 servings.

HOT CHOCOLATE SOUFFLÉ

butter
granulated sugar
1 cup milk
2 squares unsweetened chocolate
⅓ cup flour

¼ teaspoon salt
4 eggs, separated
1 teaspoon vanilla extract
¼ teaspoon almond extract

1

About 45 minutes before serving: Preheat oven to 425° F. With butter, liberally grease 1½-quart casserole; sprinkle bottom and sides with a little sugar until coated.

2

In double boiler, heat ½ cup of the milk with chocolate until melted; beat until smooth. Stir rest of milk into flour and salt; stir into chocolate. Cook, stirring, until very thick. Remove from heat; beat until smooth. Add egg yolks, one by one, beating after each addition until smooth. Cover; let stand.

3

With electric mixer, beat egg whites until they form soft peaks when beater is raised; slowly add ⅓ cup sugar, continuing to beat until stiff. Fold in yolk mixture and extracts. Pour into casserole. Bake, uncovered, 22 to 27 minutes. When 22 minutes are up, insert knife part way into center of soufflé; if it comes out clean, soufflé is done. If any soufflé adheres to knife, bake 5 minutes more.

Serve at once with soft ice cream, or whipped cream. Makes 6 servings.

<big>F</big>illing the whole house with its fragrance as it steams, this traditional Christmas delight is a pudding Tiny Tim himself would have approved of

FLUFFY STEAMED FIG PUDDING

1 pound dried figs	1 teaspoon cinnamon
1¾ cups milk or liquefied nonfat dry milk	¾ teaspoon salt
	3 eggs
1½ cups sifted all-purpose flour	1½ cups ground suet
2½ teaspoons double-acting baking powder	1½ cups fresh bread crumbs
	3 tablespoons grated orange peel
1 cup granulated sugar	
1 teaspoon nutmeg	

1

About 3 hours before serving: With scissors, snip stems from figs. Into double boiler, cut figs in small pieces; add milk; cook, covered, 20 minutes. Sift flour, baking powder, sugar, nutmeg, cinnamon, salt. In bowl, beat eggs; add suet, bread crumbs, peel, fig mixture, then flour mixture; mix well.

2

Turn into well-greased 2-quart mold; cover tightly. Place on trivet in deep kettle. Add enough boiling water to come halfway up sides of mold. Steam, covered, 2 hours, or until done. Let stand 2 minutes before removing from mold.

3

Serve with hard sauce, or vanilla ice cream, softened. Makes about 10 servings.

To Do Ahead: Make pudding several days ahead. After removing it from mold, cool; refrigerate. To serve, wrap pudding in foil; bake at 325° F. about 1 hour or until hot. Or steam in same mold 1 hour.

For a Flaming Pudding: For large pudding, heat ½ cup brandy until lukewarm; for individual puddings, heat 2 teaspoons brandy per pudding. Immediately pour brandy over and around hot pudding. Touch lighted match to brandy; carry to table ablaze.

Or soak cubes of sugar in lemon extract; place around pudding; immediately light with match.

cookies
&
candies

As much fun to make as they are to eat, these are also wonderful for holiday giving—if, that is, you can prevent your family from devouring them first

CHOCOLATE-CHIP OATMEAL COOKIES

¾ cup all-purpose flour
½ teaspoon salt
½ teaspoon baking soda
½ cup soft shortening
 6 tablespoons brown sugar
 6 tablespoons granulated sugar

1 egg
½ cup chopped walnuts
 1 6-ounce package semisweet-
   chocolate pieces (1 cup)
 1 cup uncooked rolled oats
½ teaspoon vanilla extract

1

Several days ahead: Preheat oven to 375° F. Sift flour with salt and soda. With electric mixer at medium speed, thoroughly mix shortening, sugars and egg until very light and fluffy.

2

With spoon, stir in ¼ teaspoon water, walnuts, chocolate, oats, flour mixture and vanilla, just until mixed. Drop by teaspoonfuls onto ungreased cookie sheet. Bake 12 minutes; cool on racks. Makes 5 dozen.

Make these gaily decorated cookies up to 3 weeks ahead of time; they store beautifully

GUMDROP COOKIES

3½ cups sifted all-purpose flour
 1 teaspoon baking soda
 1 teaspoon cream of tartar
dash of salt
 1 cup butter or margarine

1 cup granulated sugar
1 egg
1 teaspoon vanilla extract
tiny pastel gumdrops, halved

1

Several days or up to 3 weeks ahead: Sift flour with baking soda, cream of tartar and salt. In large bowl, with electric mixer at medium speed, beat butter with sugar and egg until fluffy. Stir in vanilla extract and flour mixture, forming dough. Wrap in waxed paper; chill 2 hours.

2

Preheat oven to 375° F. On lightly floured surface, with floured stockinette-covered rolling pin, roll half of dough to ¼-inch thickness; with fluted 2¾-inch cookie cutter, cut out cookies; remove to ungreased cookie sheet. Decorate with gumdrops; repeat. Bake 10 minutes or until golden. Cool on cookie sheet 10 minutes; remove to rack; cool. Store in container with loose-fitting cover. Makes about 3 dozen.

CHOCOLATE-CHIP OATMEAL COOKIES
GUMDROP COOKIES
HOLIDAY POINSETTIAS
CONFETTI CRISPS
PECAN FINGERS

APRICOT-CHEESE PASTRY HEARTS

M

elt-in-your-mouth cream-
cheese pastries with a filling of apricot preserves. Mmm!

APRICOT-CHEESE PASTRY HEARTS

2 cups all-purpose flour
¼ teaspoon salt
1 cup butter or margarine

1 8-ounce package cream cheese
apricot or raspberry preserves
2 eggs, beaten

1

Day before or early in day: Into medium bowl, sift flour and salt. With
pastry blender or 2 knives used scissor-fashion, cut butter and cheese in
small pieces; work into flour until all is well blended. Shape into ball;
wrap in waxed paper; refrigerate.

2

At least 2 hours before serving: Lightly grease 2 cookie sheets. Preheat
oven to 400° F. On floured surface, roll out dough ⅛-inch thick; with 3″
by 2¾″ heart-shaped cookie cutter (or 3-inch round cutter), cut out
hearts. Remove trimmings; reroll and cut out. Arrange half of hearts on
cookie sheets. In center of each, place 1 scant teaspoonful of preserves.

Brush edges with egg; cover each with another cut-out heart; with fork, press edges together. Brush tops with beaten egg; sprinkle with granulated sugar, if desired. Bake 12 minutes, or until golden; remove to rack; cool. Makes about 2½ dozen.

BIG HEART: Roll out dough into six 9-inch circles; with sharp knife, cut out 6 large hearts or other design, as pictured. Over three of hearts, spread preserves to within ½ inch of edge. Brush edges with beaten egg. Top each with second pastry heart, pressing edges together in scalloped effect. Place small cut-outs on top, if desired. Brush top with beaten egg; transfer to cookie sheets with large spatula. Bake 15 minutes, or until golden; remove to rack; cool. Brush tops with preserves, if desired. Cut each into eight wedges. Makes 24 servings.

A s pretty as the plant they're named for, these coconut-butterscotch cookies taste great too

HOLIDAY POINSETTIAS (pictured on page 197)

3 cups sifted all-purpose flour
1 teaspoon salt
2 cups sifted confectioners' sugar
1 cup butter or margarine, softened
2 eggs

2 teaspoons vanilla extract
1 cup flaked or cookie coconut
1 6-ounce package butterscotch pieces
1 4-ounce jar candied cherries

1

Anytime up to 2 weeks ahead: Sift together flour and salt; set aside.

2

In large bowl, with electric mixer at medium speed, beat confectioners' sugar with butter until light and fluffy. Beat in eggs and vanilla; add flour mixture until thoroughly mixed. Stir in coconut, and ¾ cup of the butterscotch pieces. Cover; refrigerate until firm.

3

Preheat oven to 375° F. With hands, roll level tablespoonfuls of dough into balls; arrange them, 2 inches apart, on greased cookie sheets. Flatten each with bottom of glass that has been dipped in granulated sugar. Place butterscotch piece in center of each cookie. Cut each cherry into 8 wedges; on each cookie, arrange 5 cherry wedges as pictured. Bake poinsettias 10 to 12 minutes, or until lightly browned around edges; cool on rack. Makes about 4½ dozen.

CONFETTI CRISPS (pictured on page 197)

1½ cups sifted all-purpose flour
½ teaspoon baking soda
¾ teaspoon salt
½ cup soft shortening

1 cup granulated sugar
1 egg
2 teaspoons vanilla extract
nonpareils

1

Several days before serving: Sift together flour, baking soda and salt.

2

In large bowl, with electric mixer at medium speed, mix shortening, sugar, egg and vanilla until creamy. Stir in flour mixture with wooden spoon; mix well. Turn dough onto large piece of waxed paper. Shape into roll 2 inches in diameter. Coat outside of roll with nonpareils. Refrigerate until firm enough to slice.

3

Preheat oven to 375° F. Slice dough ¼-inch thick. Place on ungreased cookie sheet. Bake 10 minutes or until golden. Cool on rack. Makes 4 dozen.

PECAN SUGARS: Omit nonpareils. Make as above, but decrease sugar to ½ cup. Add ½ cup packed brown sugar. Substitute almond extract for vanilla. Top each unbaked cookie with pecan half. Sprinkle baked cookies with granulated sugar.

Not only *may* you make these toffee bars ahead, you should—they are at their very best after storage, in a tightly covered jar, for at least 3 days

TOFFEE BARS

1 cup butter or margarine,
  softened
1 cup granulated sugar
2 cups sifted all-purpose flour

1 egg, separated
1 teaspoon vanilla extract
½ cup finely chopped walnuts

1

Several days ahead: Preheat oven to 275° F. In large bowl, with electric mixer at medium speed, cream butter with sugar. Beat in flour, egg yolk and vanilla until well blended. Spread evenly in bottom of well-greased 15½″ by 10½″ by 1″ jelly-roll pan. Brush top with egg white and sprinkle with nuts.

2

Bake 1 hour and 10 minutes or until golden. Immediately cut into 50 bars and remove from pan to cool on rack. Store, tightly covered, for at least 3 days before serving. Makes about 4 dozen cookies.

Like apple pie, brownies are almost everybody's favorite. These have a rich chocolate flavor and are tender, light and studded with walnuts

---

BROWNIES

¾ cup sifted cake flour
½ teaspoon double-acting baking
    powder
¾ teaspoon salt
1 cup granulated sugar
½ cup soft shortening
2 eggs, unbeaten

1 teaspoon vanilla extract
2 to 2½ squares unsweetened
    chocolate, melted
1 cup chopped walnuts, almonds,
    pecans, Brazil nuts, pistachio
    nuts or peanuts

1

Early in day: Preheat oven to 350° F. Grease well 8″ by 8″ by 2″ baking pan. Sift flour, baking powder, salt.

2

In large bowl, with electric mixer at medium speed, gradually add sugar to shortening, beating until very light and fluffy. Add eggs, vanilla; beat until smooth. Mix in chocolate, then flour mixture and nuts. (If desired, save half of nuts to sprinkle on top of batter before baking.)

3

Turn into pan. Bake 30 to 35 minutes, or until done. Cool slightly; cut into squares or bars; sprinkle with confectioners' sugar, if desired. Store right in pan. Makes 16 squares.

FRUIT: For part or all of nuts, substitute chopped raisins, pitted dates, or dates and nuts.

CRUNCHY COOKIES

1½ cups sifted all-purpose flour
½ teaspoon baking soda
1 teaspoon salt
1 teaspoon cinnamon
½ cup soft shortening
½ cup granulated sugar
½ cup honey

1 egg
¼ cup milk
½ cup dark or golden raisins
½ cup coarsely chopped walnuts
4 shredded-wheat biscuits, crumbled

1

Several days ahead: Sift flour with baking soda, salt and cinnamon. Preheat oven to 375° F.

2

In large bowl, with electric mixer at medium speed, beat shortening with sugar, honey and egg until well blended. Beat flour mixture into sugar mixture alternately with milk. Stir in raisins, walnuts and shredded-wheat crumbs. Drop dough, by heaping teaspoonfuls, onto greased cookie sheets. Bake 12 to 15 minutes or until done. Cool on racks. Store in tightly covered container. Makes about 4 dozen.

Tender coconut macaroons that have no need of baking—who wouldn't vote for *them?*

QUICK MACAROONS

⅓ cup evaporated milk, undiluted
2 tablespoons butter
¾ cup granulated sugar

½ teaspoon vanilla extract
1 cup flaked coconut
½ cup coarsely broken pecans
1½ cups cornflakes

1

Early in day: In large saucepan, combine evaporated milk, butter and sugar. Cook, stirring constantly, until mixture comes to full rolling boil. Lower heat; continue to boil, stirring, 2 minutes. Remove from heat.

2

Quickly stir in vanilla, coconut, pecans and cornflakes, making sure all pieces are well coated with milk mixture. Using two teaspoons, quickly drop mixture in mounds, onto waxed-paper-lined cookie sheet. Refrigerate until firm. Makes about 12.

QUICK MACAROONS
MUFFIN-PAN CRISPIES
CRESCENT MELTAWAYS
SHORTBREAD SANDWICHES
SURPRISE COOKIE BALLS

CRESCENT MELTAWAYS (pictured on page 203)

1 8-ounce package creamed
  cottage cheese
1 cup butter or margarine
2 cups sifted all-purpose flour
¼ cup melted butter or

  margarine
¾ cup packed light brown sugar
dash cinnamon
¾ cup finely-chopped walnuts
  1 egg yolk, unbeaten

1

Day before or early in day: In medium bowl, blend cheese with 1 cup butter. Sift in flour, then blend until dough forms ball.

2

Preheat oven to 400° F. Divide dough in thirds. On lightly floured surface, roll out one-third of dough into ⅛-inch-thick circle. Brush with some of melted butter; sprinkle with ¼ cup of the brown sugar, cinnamon and ¼ cup of the chopped nuts. Cut into 16 pie-shaped pieces. Beginning at outer edge, roll up each piece tightly; place, point side down, on greased cookie sheet.

3

Beat egg yolk with 2 tablespoons water; use to brush tops of cookies. Bake 20 minutes or until golden. Cool on racks. Repeat the procedure with other two-thirds of dough. Makes 4 dozen.

---

ou pile a spicy oats mixture into muffin pans, bake 15 minutes, then add a brown-sugar sauce and bake some more. Now doesn't *that* sound good?

MUFFIN-PAN CRISPIES (pictured on page 203)

butter or margarine, softened
light brown sugar
¼ teaspoon salt
½ teaspoon double-acting baking
  powder

1 teaspoon vanilla extract
1½ cups uncooked rolled oats
  1 tablespoon milk
¼ teaspoon cinnamon
dash nutmeg

1

Several days ahead: Preheat oven to 350° F. In medium bowl, with mixer at medium speed, mix ¼ cup butter with ⅓ cup packed light brown sugar, salt, baking powder and vanilla until mixture is smooth. Stir in rolled oats, then milk; mix until well blended.

Into each of 12 ungreased muffin-pan cups, measuring 2 inches across bottom, lightly pile about 1½ tablespoonfuls of rolled-oat mixture; with fork, very gently level off top of each. Bake for 15 minutes.

3

Meanwhile, in saucepan, melt ¼ cup butter; stir in ⅓ cup packed brown sugar, ¼ cup hot water, cinnamon and nutmeg. Heat 2 minutes, stirring constantly. Spoon about 1½ teaspoons brown-sugar sauce over each lined muffin pan. Return to oven for 15 minutes more.

With thin-bladed spatula, very carefully loosen edges of each cookie from pan all around. Cool 5 minutes; carefully remove from pans; finish cooling on paper towels on rack. Store in tightly covered container. These cookies keep well. Makes 1 dozen.

Strawberry preserves fill a light, crisp cookie made "short" by a whole cup of butter

---

SHORTBREAD SANDWICHES (pictured on page 203)

2 *cups sifted all-purpose flour*	1 *cup butter*
¼ *teaspoon double-acting baking powder*	½ *cup confectioners' sugar* *granulated sugar*
¼ *teaspoon salt*	¼ *cup strawberry preserves*

1

Several days ahead: Sift flour with baking powder and salt. In small bowl, mix butter with confectioners' sugar until very light and fluffy. Mix in flour mixture. Refrigerate until easy to handle (about 1 hour).

2

Preheat oven to 350° F. On lightly floured surface, roll dough ¼ inch thick. Cut into 1¾-inch circles. Place 1 inch apart on ungreased cookie sheets. Bake 20 minutes or until done. Remove cookies to racks.

3

Lightly sprinkle half of cookies with granulated sugar. Spread strawberry preserves evenly over the remaining cookies; top each with one sugared cookie, sandwich fashion. Makes 30 cookies.

BRANDY BALLS

R ich sweet morsels with a tantalizing aroma, these make marvelous Christmas presents. For dramatic giving, heap them in a crystal brandy snifter

BRANDY BALLS

2 7¼-ounce packages vanilla
  wafers, finely crushed
½ cup honey
⅓ cup brandy

⅓ cup white rum
4 cups walnuts, finely ground
  granulated sugar

1

Several days ahead: In medium bowl, mix together cookie crumbs, honey, brandy, rum and ground walnuts.

2

Shape into round, bite-size balls; roll in granulated sugar. Wrap each in plastic wrap. The longer they are kept, the better the flavor! Store in container. Makes about 5 dozen.

SURPRISE COOKIE BALLS (pictured on page 203)

1 6-ounce package semisweet-
  chocolate pieces (1 cup)
3 tablespoons light corn syrup
2 teaspoons instant coffee
3 cups sifted confectioners' sugar
1 cup chopped walnuts

about 3 dozen packaged vanilla
  wafers, finely crushed (1¾
  cups)
1 large nutted candy bar
confectioners' sugar

1

Several days before serving: In double boiler, over hot, *not boiling,* water, melt chocolate pieces; remove from heat. Stir in corn syrup, coffee dissolved in ⅓ cup hot water, 3 cups sugar, walnuts and crumbs; mix well.

2

Cut candy bar into 4 dozen small pieces. Around each piece, mold some of chocolate mixture into 1-inch ball; roll in confectioners' sugar. Store in covered container a day or so to ripen. Makes about 5 dozen.

CHOCO-ORANGE BALLS: Substitute ⅓ cup orange juice for coffee and hot water.

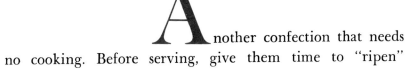

nother confection that needs no cooking. Before serving, give them time to "ripen"

WALNUT BOURBON BALLS

5 dozen packaged vanilla wafers,
  finely crushed (2½ cups)
2 tablespoons cocoa
1 cup confectioners' sugar
1 cup finely chopped walnuts, or

walnuts and flaked coconut
3 tablespoons light corn syrup
¼ cup bourbon
confectioners' sugar

1

Several days before serving: In medium bowl, combine wafer crumbs, cocoa, 1 cup confectioners' sugar, nuts. Add corn syrup, bourbon; mix well.

2

Form into 1-inch balls; roll in confectioners' sugar. Store in covered container a day or so to ripen; these keep very well. Makes 3½ dozen.

PECAN FINGERS (pictured on page 197)

2¼ cups all-purpose flour
½ teaspoon double-acting
    baking powder
dash salt
  1 cup butter, softened

¾ cup granulated sugar
1 egg, unbeaten
1 teaspoon almond extract
1 egg white, slightly beaten
1½ cups chopped pecans

1

At least a day ahead: In medium bowl, sift flour with baking powder and salt.

2

In large bowl, with mixer at medium speed, beat butter with sugar until light and fluffy. Beat in egg and almond extract. Gradually add flour mixture, beating until well blended.

3

Preheat oven to 400° F. Onto ungreased cookie sheets, with cookie press and ribbon disk, press out dough into 3-inch strips. Brush with egg white; sprinkle with pecans. Repeat until all dough is used. Bake 9 to 11 minutes or until lightly browned at edges.

4

With broad spatula remove to rack to cool. Store in tightly covered container. Makes 6 dozen.

Among our best-liked cookies is our cakelike version of the fruit- and nut-filled German favorites, Lebkuchen. The topping is a snowy glaze

LEBKUCHEN

2¼ cups sifted all-purpose flour
½ teaspoon salt
  1 teaspoon double-acting
    baking powder
½ teaspoon ground cloves
  1 teaspoon cinnamon
  1 cup coarsely chopped walnuts
  2 4-ounce jars diced mixed

    candied fruits
3 eggs
1 egg yolk
1½ cups packed dark brown
    sugar
½ cup strong coffee or sherry
Snowy Glaze (opposite)

1

Several days before serving: Preheat oven to 375° F. Sift flour, salt, baking powder, cloves, cinnamon; mix with nuts, fruits. Grease 15½" by 10½" by 1" jelly-roll pan.

2

With electric mixer at high speed, or with rotary beater, beat eggs and egg yolk until thick and lemon-colored; gradually beat in sugar. With spoon, thoroughly blend in coffee and flour mixture. Turn into pan.

3

Bake 25 minutes or until cake tester inserted at several points comes out clean. Cool in pan on rack.

4

Frost with Snowy Glaze. Before frosting dries, with wet knife, mark into 2" by 2½" bars; when dry, cut. Store in tight container with an apple wedge to keep bars soft. Makes about 2½ dozen.

SNOWY GLAZE: Mix 1 cup sifted confectioners' sugar with 2 to 3 tablespoons warm milk, ¼ teaspoon almond or vanilla extract.

With the simplicity of perfection, these golden drop cookies are made in minutes

---

ORANGE CRISPIES

---

1 cup soft shortening	*1 egg, unbeaten*
½ teaspoon salt	*1½ teaspoons orange extract*
granulated sugar	*1½ cups sifted all-purpose flour*

1

Early in day: Preheat oven to 375° F. In medium bowl, with electric mixer, cream shortening with salt until light and fluffy, while gradually adding 1 cup sugar. Add egg; beat well. Blend in orange extract, then flour. Onto ungreased cookie sheets, drop rounded tablespoonfuls of dough, 2 inches apart. Bake 10 minutes, or until edges are light brown. Let stand 1 or 2 minutes before removing. While cookies are warm, sprinkle with granulated sugar. Makes 4 dozen.

A delightfully different cookie from Norway, brandy-flavored fattigmand are rolled paper-thin, fried a delicate brown, then dusted with sugar

FATTIGMAND

3 eggs
3 tablespoons heavy cream
¼ cup granulated sugar
1½ tablespoons melted shortening
1 tablespoon brandy

½ teaspoon salt
½ teaspoon ground cardamom
about 3 cups sifted all-purpose flour
salad oil
confectioners' sugar

1

Early in day: In medium bowl, mix eggs thoroughly with cream and sugar. Add melted shortening, brandy, salt, cardamom and 2 cups flour; mix. Stir in enough additional flour to make stiff dough. Wrap in waxed paper; chill 1 hour or longer.

2

Into deep saucepan, pour 2 inches of salad oil. Heat to 365° F. on deep fat thermometer. On lightly floured surface, roll half of dough paper-thin. Cut into 3-inch-long diamonds. Make slit in center of each; pull one corner through slit. Fry till delicate brown. Drain on paper towels. Cool. Dust with confectioners' sugar. Repeat. Makes 8 dozen.

CASHEW-CARAMEL YUMMIES

¾ cup sifted all-purpose flour
½ teaspoon double-acting baking powder
¼ teaspoon salt
2 eggs, slightly beaten
½ cup granulated sugar
brown sugar

½ cup chopped salted cashew nuts
2 tablespoons melted butter or margarine
1½ tablespoons light cream
⅓ cup chopped salted cashew nuts

1

Early in day: Preheat oven to 350° F. Sift flour, baking powder, salt.

2

In small bowl, combine eggs, granulated sugar and ½ cup packed brown sugar. Then blend in ½ cup nuts and flour mixture. Turn mixture into greased 9" by 9" by 2" pan. Bake 20 minutes or until crust springs back when lightly touched with finger.

3

Meanwhile, make Cashew Topping: Into butter, stir ¼ cup packed brown sugar, cream, ⅓ cup nuts. Spread immediately on baked cookie mixture, covering top completely. Place under broiler about 1 minute, or until topping bubbles and is light brown. While cookies are warm, cut into bars; cool thoroughly in pan. Makes about 3 dozen.

Filled with maraschino cherries, walnuts and marshmallows, then drizzled with chocolate sauce—is it any mystery how these cookies got their name?

CHOCOLATE SUNDAE COOKIES

⅔ cup packed brown sugar
soft shortening
  1 egg
  ½ teaspoon baking soda
  ½ teaspoon salt
1½ cups sifted all-purpose flour
  ¼ cup maraschino-cherry juice
  2 tablespoons milk
  2 squares unsweetened

chocolate, melted
  1 teaspoon vanilla extract
  ¼ cup chopped maraschino
    cherries
  ½ cup chopped walnuts
about 2 dozen large
    marshmallows, halved
  1 6-ounce package semisweet-
    chocolate pieces

1

Up to 1 week before serving: Preheat oven to 350° F. In large bowl, with electric mixer at medium speed, blend brown sugar with ½ cup shortening. Beat in egg, then baking soda, salt and flour until blended; add cherry juice, milk, melted chocolate and vanilla; beat well. Stir in cherries and walnuts.

2

Drop by heaping teaspoonfuls onto ungreased cookie sheets. Bake 12 to 15 minutes. As soon as cookies come from oven, top each with marshmallow half, cut side down; cool on racks.

3

In double boiler, over hot, *not boiling,* water, melt semisweet chocolate with ¼ cup shortening. Drizzle over marshmallows and cookies; dry on racks. Store in airtight container. Makes about 4 dozen cookies.

ALMOND ROLLS

2/3 cup canned blanched almonds, finely ground
1/2 cup butter or margarine
1/2 cup granulated sugar

2 tablespoons milk
1 tablespoon flour
sifted confectioners' sugar

1

*Early in day:** Preheat oven to 350° F. Grease and flour well two cookie sheets. In large skillet, combine all ingredients except confectioners' sugar; heat stirring, over low heat until butter is melted and mixture is mushy. Drop by level tablespoonfuls, only 4 cookies to the cookie sheet, at least 3 inches apart.

2

Bake, 1 sheet at a time, about 5 or 6 minutes or until golden. Let cool on sheet just a minute or so. With wide spatula, remove each cookie; turn over and quickly roll up around handle of a wooden spoon; cool. (If cookie gets too hard to roll, reheat in oven a minute to soften.) Let cookie sheet cool before using again. Makes 30 rolls.

*Mixture is hard to handle on a rainy day.

GRANDMOTHER NEWMAN'S SPICE COOKIES

4 cups sifted all-purpose flour
1½ teaspoons baking soda
1½ teaspoons cinnamon
½ teaspoon nutmeg
¼ teaspoon cloves

1 cup butter or margarine
granulated sugar
2 eggs
1 tablespoon milk
1 cup dried currants or raisins

1

Up to 2 weeks ahead: Sift together flour, baking soda, cinnamon, nutmeg and cloves.

2

In large bowl, with electric mixer at medium speed, beat butter with 1½ cups sugar until light and fluffy; beat in eggs until well blended. With mixer at low speed, beat in milk, then flour mixture. Stir in currants. Shape dough into ball; wrap in waxed paper; chill.

3

Preheat oven to 375° F. On floured surface, roll dough as thin as possible; sprinkle with sugar. With pastry wheel or knife, cut dough into 2-inch diamonds. Bake on cookie sheets 8 minutes or until very lightly browned; cool on racks. Store, loosely covered. Makes 10 dozen cookies.

GRANDMOTHER NEWMAN'S SPICE COOKIES
LUSCIOUS APRICOT SQUARES
ALMOND ROLLS
CINNAMON STARS

LUSCIOUS APRICOT SQUARES (pictured on page 212)

⅔ cup dried apricots
½ cup butter or margarine,
  softened
¼ cup granulated sugar
1⅓ cups sifted all-purpose flour
½ teaspoon double-acting
  baking powder

¼ teaspoon salt
1 cup packed light brown sugar
2 eggs
½ cup chopped walnuts
½ teaspoon vanilla extract
confectioners' sugar

1

Early in day: Cook apricots as label directs; drain and chop finely.

2

Preheat oven to 350° F. In large bowl, cream butter and granulated sugar; stir in 1 cup of the flour until crumbly; pack mixture into greased 8″ by 8″ by 2″ cake pan. Bake 25 minutes or until lightly browned.

3

Meanwhile, sift together ⅓ cup flour, baking powder and salt. In large bowl, with electric mixer at medium speed, beat brown sugar and eggs until blended; beat in flour mixture, walnuts, vanilla and apricots. Spread over baked layer and bake 25 minutes more or until golden.

4

Cool on rack; sprinkle with confectioners' sugar. Cut into squares. Store tightly covered. Makes 16.

lmond macaroons with extra appeal—a spicy cinnamon-lemon flavor and a star shape

CINNAMON STARS (pictured on page 212)

3 large egg whites
confectioners' sugar
2 cups ground blanched almonds

1 teaspoon cinnamon
½ teaspoon grated lemon peel

1

Several days ahead: In medium bowl, with electric mixer at high speed, beat egg whites until stiff but not dry; gradually beat in 2 cups confectioners' sugar. Spoon out ¾ cup for frosting stars; set aside.

2

To rest of mixture, blend in almonds, cinnamon, lemon peel and ½ cup more confectioners' sugar. Refrigerate until "dough" is workable. Preheat oven to 350° F.

3

On waxed paper, well dusted with confectioners' sugar, pat out one-third of "dough" and generously coat top with confectioners' sugar. Cover with waxed paper and roll out ⅛ inch thick. Peel off top paper; with well-floured, 2¾-inch star cutter, cut cookies. With pancake turner, place stars on well greased cookie sheet. Bake 10 minutes. Cool on rack. Repeat with remaining "dough."

4

Frost cookies with reserved meringue. Return to 325° F. oven for 5 minutes or until meringue is set but still white. Cool and store, tightly covered. Makes 3 dozen cookies.

---

s crisp and delicate as their name promises, these are perfect for tea parties

LACY RAISIN WAFERS

¾ *cup sifted all-purpose flour*	½ *cup salad oil*
½ *teaspoon baking soda*	1 *cup packed brown sugar*
½ *teaspoon salt*	1 *teaspoon vanilla extract*
¼ *teaspoon cinnamon*	1½ *cups uncooked rolled oats*
¼ *teaspoon nutmeg*	½ *cup chopped nuts*
¾ *cup dark raisins*	

1

Early in day: Sift flour, soda, salt, cinnamon, nutmeg. Rinse and drain raisins; mix with salad oil, ½ cup water; mix in sugar, vanilla, oats, nuts, then flour mixture. Refrigerate 1 hour.

2

Preheat oven to 350° F. Drop dough by teaspoonfuls, about 2 inches apart, onto greased cookie sheet. Bake 10 to 12 minutes or until crisp around edges. Makes 3½ dozen.

CHOCOLATE-DRIZZLED PECAN PENUCHE

2 cups granulated sugar
2 cups packed light brown sugar
½ cup light cream
½ cup milk
3 tablespoons butter or
  margarine

1 cup coarsely chopped pecans
1½ teaspoons vanilla extract
½ cup semisweet-chocolate
  pieces
24 pecan halves

1

2 or 3 days before serving: Butter sides *only* of heavy 2½-quart sauce-pan. Add sugars, cream, milk and butter. Over medium heat, stir just until sugars dissolve and mixture boils. (Don't let candy coat sides of saucepan—it may become granular.) Boil mixture, without stirring, until candy thermometer reads 238° F., or until a little dropped in cold water makes soft ball. Immediately remove from heat; cool to 110° F. without stirring.

2

Add chopped pecans and vanilla; with electric mixer at high speed, beat until mixture becomes thick and begins to lose its gloss; watch carefully. Quickly pour into buttered 8″ by 8″ by 2″ baking pan, spread-ing evenly over bottom of pan. When somewhat firm and still warm, cut into 24 pieces with sharp knife; cool.

3

Melt chocolate in double boiler over hot, *not boiling,* water. With teaspoon, drizzle chocolate over top of candy. Place pecan half on each piece. Store in tightly covered container. Makes 24 candies.

A superb nibbler with after-dinner coffee. Also try orange peel, candied the same way

CANDIED GRAPEFRUIT PEEL

2 grapefruit
granulated sugar

½ cup light corn syrup

1

2 or 3 days ahead: Cut peel from each grapefruit into 4 lengthwise sec-tions. (If white membrane is very thick, remove some of it; otherwise leave intact.) Cover peel with cold water; bring to boil. Boil 10 minutes; drain. Repeat this cooking and draining 3 times.

2

Cut peel into thin strips. In 3-quart saucepan, combine 1 cup sugar, corn syrup and 1 cup water. Stir over low heat until sugar is dissolved. Add peel; boil gently about 40 minutes or until most of syrup is absorbed. Drain in coarse strainer or colander.

3

Roll peel, few pieces at a time, in granulated sugar. Arrange in single layer; let dry about 48 hours. Store in covered container. Makes about ½ pound.

CANDIED ORANGE PEEL: Substitute 6 thick-skinned oranges for grapefruit. Increase sugar to 2 cups. Decrease corn syrup to 2 teaspoons. Boil peel 5 minutes each time instead of 10. Makes about 1½ pounds.

Made with marshmallow cream, this special fudge is then poured over marshmallows

---

FUDGE DELIGHTFUL

¼ pound marshmallows, quartered
2 cups granulated sugar
4 teaspoons cocoa
1 cup milk

2 teaspoons butter or margarine
4 teaspoons marshmallow cream
1 teaspoon vanilla extract
1 cup chopped nuts

1

Early in day: Arrange quartered marshmallows so they cover bottom of greased 10″ by 6″ by 2″ baking dish.

2

In saucepan, combine sugar, cocoa, milk, butter. Heat, stirring, until dissolved. Bring to boil; continue cooking, without stirring, to 236° F. on candy thermometer, or until a little mixture in cold water forms soft ball.

3

Remove mixture from heat. Stir in marshmallow cream, vanilla, nuts. Beat until creamy. Pour over marshmallows. Cool. Cut into 40 pieces.

FRENCH CHOCOLATES

1 12-ounce package semisweet-chocolate pieces (2 cups)
1 cup chopped walnuts
¾ cup canned sweetened condensed milk

1 teaspoon vanilla extract
dash salt
chopped flaked coconut or walnuts, or chocolate sprinkles, for garnish

1

Early in day: In double boiler, over hot, *not boiling*, water, melt chocolate pieces. Stir in 1 cup chopped walnuts, condensed milk, vanilla extract and salt; remove from heat; cool 5 minutes or until easy to shape. With greased hands, shape into 1-inch balls. Dip balls into chopped coconut, walnuts or sprinkles. Makes 1¼ pounds.

HEAVENLY TRUFFLES: Pour mixture into greased, then waxed-paper-lined 9″ by 5″ by 3″ loaf pan. Cool several hours; when firm, cut into squares.

s sweet as sugar—because that's just what it is, in a velvety egg-white mixture. To vary the taste, add chopped walnuts, hazelnuts, or pecans

LYNN'S HEAVENLY DIVINITY

3 cups granulated sugar
½ cup light corn syrup

2 egg whites
1 teaspoon vanilla extract

1

*1 week or more ahead:** In medium saucepan, boil sugar, syrup, ½ cup water until a little forms soft ball when dropped in cold water.

2

Meanwhile, in medium bowl, with electric mixer at high speed, beat egg whites until stiff. Pour half of syrup into whites, beating continually. Return other half of syrup to heat and boil until a little forms hard ball when dropped in cold water. Pour syrup into egg-mixture, beating until mixture is quite firm and stands in peaks; fold in vanilla. When spoonful dropped onto waxed paper holds its shape, divinity is ready; drop by heaping teaspoonfuls onto paper. Cool; store in tightly covered container. Makes about 60 candies.

NUTTY DIVINITY: Stir in 1 cup chopped nuts, when adding vanilla.

*Avoid making on a humid or rainy day as candy will not harden.

NUT CRUNCH

1¼ cups granulated sugar
¾ cup butter or margarine
1½ teaspoons salt
½ cup unblanched almonds
½ teaspoon baking soda
½ cup blanched almonds

½ cup chopped walnuts (or
  Brazil nuts)
⅓ cup semisweet-chocolate pieces,
  melted
½ cup finely chopped nuts

1

Several days ahead: In large, heavy saucepan, mix sugar, butter, salt, unblanched almonds and ¼ cup water. Boil, stirring often, until mixture reaches 290° F. on candy thermometer or until a little mixture dropped in cold water becomes brittle.

2

Quickly stir in soda, blanched almonds and chopped walnuts; pour into greased 15½″ by 10½″ by 1″ pan. Spread with melted chocolate; sprinkle with finely chopped nuts. Cool; break up. Makes 1½ pounds.

Cookies that fill the kitchen with the fresh fragrance of sugaring-off time in Vermont

MAPLE KISSES (pictured on page 219)

1 cup packed light brown sugar
½ cup granulated sugar
¼ cup light corn syrup
½ cup evaporated milk,
  undiluted

1 tablespoon butter or
  margarine
1 teaspoon maple flavor
1½ cups chopped walnuts

1

Up to 1 week ahead: In medium saucepan over very low heat, cook sugars, corn syrup and evaporated milk, stirring constantly, until mixture reaches 235° F. on candy thermometer or until a little dropped in cold water forms soft ball. (Takes about 30 minutes.)

2

Remove from heat; with spoon, beat in butter, maple flavor and nuts. Quickly drop mixture by teaspoonfuls onto waxed paper; cool. When set, store in tightly covered container. Makes about 24.

PEANUT KISSES: **Prepare recipe as above but use chopped salted peanuts instead of walnuts.**

BUTTERSCOTCH WAFERS

½ cup granulated sugar
¼ cup light corn syrup
1 tablespoon butter or

margarine
½ teaspoon vanilla extract

1

Make ahead, if desired: In 2-quart saucepan, combine sugar, corn syrup, ¼ cup water. Cook over low heat, stirring, until sugar is dissolved.

2

Continue gentle cooking, without stirring, until mixture reaches 265° F. on candy thermometer or until a little mixture dropped in cold water forms very hard ball. Add butter; cook to 290° F. or until a little mixture dropped in cold water becomes brittle.

3

Remove from heat; add vanilla; drop, from regular teaspoon, onto greased pan. When firm, remove with spatula. Makes about 2 dozen.

An appropriate finale to our all-time favorite recipes is this fudge that tastes just as marvelous as everybody, including you, remembers it

OLD-FASHIONED FUDGE

2 cups granulated sugar
1 cup milk; or ½ cup
  evaporated milk, undiluted,
  and ½ cup water
½ teaspoon salt
2 squares unsweetened

chocolate
2 tablespoons light corn syrup
2 tablespoons butter or
  margarine
½ teaspoon vanilla extract
½ cup chopped nuts

1

About 2 hours ahead: In saucepan, combine sugar, milk, salt, chocolate, corn syrup; stir over low heat until sugar dissolves. Cook gently, stirring occasionally, to 238° F. on candy thermometer or until a little mixture dropped into cold water forms soft ball. Remove from heat; drop in butter; *do not stir.*

2

Cool, without stirring, to 110° F. or until outside of saucepan feels lukewarm to hand. Add vanilla. With spoon, beat until candy loses gloss and small amount dropped from spoon holds its shape. Add nuts. Turn into greased 9″ by 5″ by 3″ loaf pan (don't scrape saucepan; leavings may be sugary) . Cool; cut. Makes 1¼ pounds.

index